Brinton Park and Sutton Common

A history of Brinton Park & the Sutton Common area with extracts from the log books of St. John's Schools

by Betty I Park

LOTTERY FUNDED

Every effort has been made to trace the copyright of all the photographs reproduced in this book.
Apologies are made for when this has proved to be impossible.

First published 2008

by Kidderminster Civic Society

in partnership with The Friends of Brinton Park

ISBN 978-0-9558945-0-3

The author has been a member of the Bewdley Historical Research Group for over 20 years and has contributed to their publications. She was a founder member of Worcestershire History Forum.

She is the author of the local history book 'Horsefair and Broadwaters'.

Designed & Printed by Veldonn Printers Ltd.
Kidderminster, Worcs, 01562 68477

ACKNOWLEDGMENTS

I would like to give sincere thanks to the following for their help and encouragement in the production of this book:

Brian Brookes and members of the Bewdley Historical Research Group for proof reading the manuscript, the staff at Kidderminster Reference Library and Bewdley Museum for assistance and the loan of photographs, Lesley Fox and staff at the Cultural, Leisure and commercial Services and all those who have generously lent their photographs and contributed their memories of past times. I am also very grateful to St. John's Schools for the use of the Log Books so carefully preserved over the years.

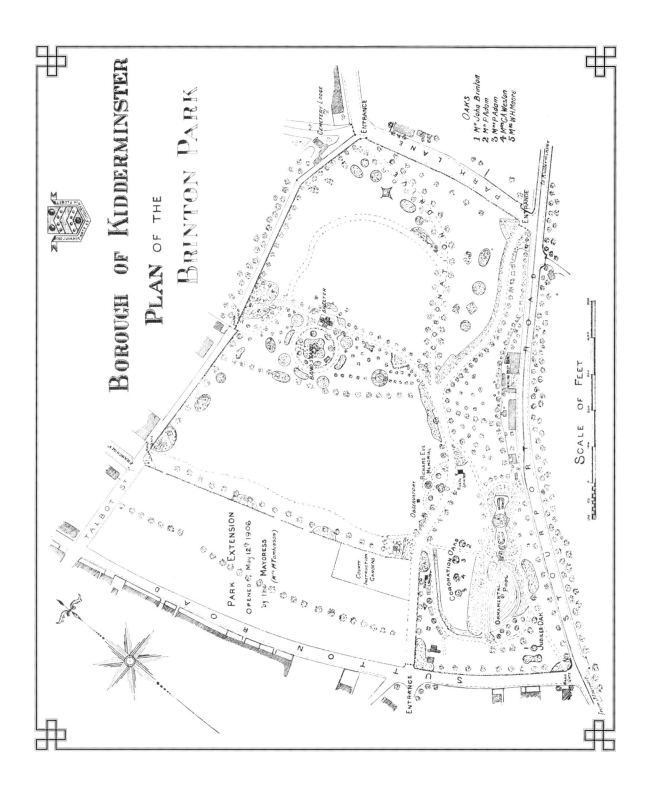

Borough of Kidderminster
Plan of the
Brinton Park

OAKS
1 Mr John Brinton
2 Mr P. Adam
3 Mrs P. Adam
4 Mrs G.A. Weston
5 Mrs W.H. Moore.

Park Extension
Opened May 12th 1906
by the Mayoress
(Mrs M Tomkinson)

SCALE OF FEET

FOREWORD

From land gifted to the town by John Brinton in 1887, in the days of Kidderminster's thriving carpet industry, and thanks to the philanthropy of Richard Eve, Brinton Park remains the centre of a community that has seen many changes throughout its existence.

Betty Park takes us on a journey through the social history of the Park, its people and the Sutton Common area. We learn about the early days and formation of Brinton Park and the creation of the surrounding area as we know it today. A fascinating insight to life in two World Wars is to be had through extracts from school log books dating back to 1862.

There is something to interest everyone with a desire to know more about local history and the way we used to live.

Brian Brookes
Chairman Friends of Brinton Park

CONTENTS

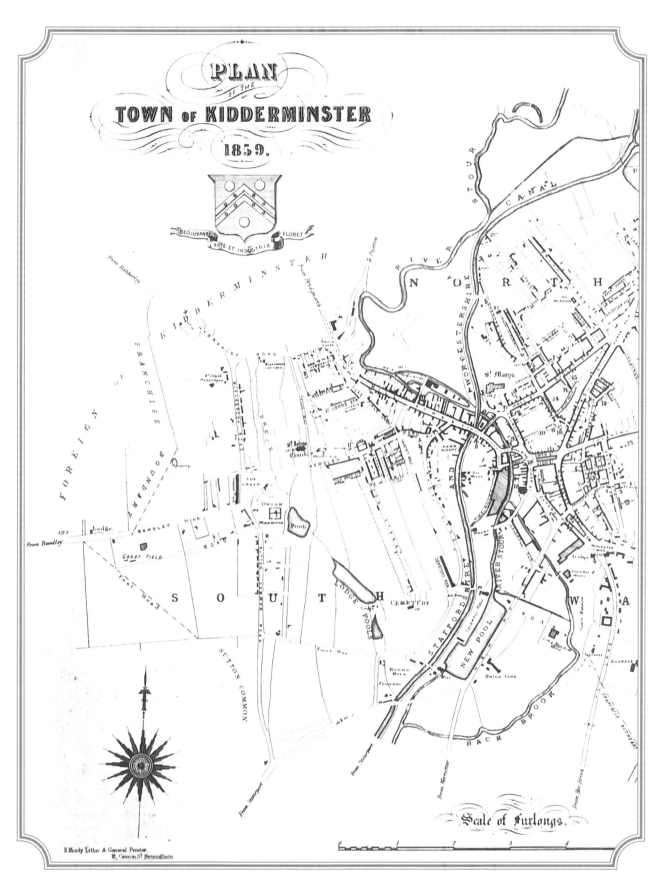

Part of the plan of Kidderminster showing the Sutton Common and Park area

# INTRODUCTION

Following the talk on "Who was Richard Eve?" by Charles Townley, past Chairman of Kidderminster Civic Society, in October 2000, interest in restoring the monument to that liberal minded thinker was raised, I was therefore delighted when Betty Park asked the Civic Society to publish her book, "A History of Brinton Park and the Sutton Common area".

I have remained involved in the consultations about the refurbishment of the Monument and the Brinton Park project and have been pleased to see the local interest volunteered through the Friends of the Brinton Park group. I wish them well for the future.

I know that Betty's easy to follow approach coupled with a detailed and methodical investigation into the history of the area will make for a fascinating read and I am so glad that we have been able to help with this project and be associated with it.

Nick Hughes

Chairman Kidderminster Civic Society

Brinton Park

Brinton Park 2006 by Jes Hamblett - Courtesy Kidderminster Reference Library

Brinton Park 2006 by Jes Hamblett - Courtesy Kidderminster Reference Library

Brinton Park

Brinton Park 2006 by Jes Hamblett - Courtesy Kidderminster Reference Library

Brinton Park 2006 by Jes Hamblett - Courtesy Kidderminster Reference Library

A HISTORY OF BRINTON PARK AND THE SUTTON COMMON AREA

This would seem to be a fitting time with the establishment of the Friends of Brinton Park, and the subsequent refurbishment and renovation of the memorial to Richard Eve, to look at the history of the Park. The Freehold of the ground was bought by John Brinton, he allowed public meetings to be held there, and subsequently gave it to the Borough for the use of the people.

This extract from Ebenezer Guest the local historian, describes how the gift of the park came about:

The People's Park

"The rest of the lane was bought by Mr. John Brinton, and called by him The People's Park, and public meetings were allowed and encouraged. Political feeling grew calmer, and in keeping with other great acts of liberality he presented it to the Corporation for public purposes, and they in gratitude have named it Brinton Park."

It was stated in the *Kidderminster Shuttle* that John Brinton D.L., J.P., had bought the land in Sutton Common alongside Sutton Lane some years before the presentation of the Deed of Gift of the Park to Kidderminster Corporation He had allowed public meetings to be held there, and on one occasion at least, it is said to have been of an "assembly of thousands". He spent £3000 upon landscape work of the 23 acres of grounds and then presented it to the Borough on **August 1st 1887**, the total value was estimated to be £7000. The booklet published to commemorate that day gives information about the ceremony and John Brinton's reasons for the gift it states: "The presentation of the Park by Mr. Brinton was regarded as a conspicuous permanent local memorial of the Jubilee of the Victorian period."

Kidderminster Shuttle August 1887

He said:

"I have long felt that, while enjoying myself in my own grounds, many persons had no such privilege to enjoy on their part. My anxiety has been for several years to try and ensure the benefit of a Public Park to the townspeople."

It is stated that little was done by the Borough to add to the attractions of the Park for some years. When the kiosk was burnt down in 1890, the site was allowed to remain unoccupied until 1896 when a new Kiosk was erected with a Bandstand on the adjoining site (it stood close to the later tennis courts). A 'Parks Committee' was then appointed and improvements were carried out.

Subsequently the Royal Salute on the occasion of Queen Victoria's Diamond Jubilee in 1897 was fired in the park. A service with 7,000 children in attendance was held in the afternoon and a grand firework display followed in the evening, when it was estimated that not less than 10,000 people were present in the park.

Richard Eve Memorial 1956
Kidderminster Reference Library

The 1906 booklet for the occasion states:

"Further improvements and additions followed in the early twentieth century. In 1902 a drinking fountain was erected by public subscription as memorial to Richard Eve. In the same year the Coronation of King Edward VIII and Queen Alexandra, besides being the occasion for local celebrations in the park, was marked by the opening of a new entrance and drive leading from the cemetery end of Park Lane and extending to Sutton Road. This was named Coronation Drive."

Mr. Brinton commissioned Mr. Meredith of Meredith and Pritchard's of Bank Buildings, a local firm of architects, to design gates for the Park Lane entrance, he also designed the pavilion, they are illustrated here. The firm still flourishes as Phipps and Pritchard, Estate Agents, having more recently moved from Bank Buildings to Worcester Street.

Ornamental Gates Erected 1905
Kidderminster Reference Library

The Commemoration booklet also informs of other earlier improvements:

In **1898** an additional entrance was made at the corner of Sutton Road and Stourport Road for the benefit of the Foley Park residents.

1902 saw the inhabitants assembled in the park to rejoice when peace was declared in South Africa (in June) they concluded the rejoicings with a huge bonfire.

On August 9th the Kidderminster diarist, William Whitcomb wrote:

"**Coronation day**. Early service then an hours ride to see the decoration round the town. went up to the Park ceremony. There was a very large crowd up there and we were just in time to see the bonfire lighted and the fireworks were let off on the hill adjacent to the Park. The Town Hall was magnificent."

After the Special Coronation Service a very long and comprehensive procession, headed by the Imperial Yeomanry made their way to the park where another Special Service was held. Entertainments were concluded with a Military Tattoo and Torchlight Procession.

In **1903** the refreshment pavilion was opened and an enclosure made around the bandstand.

The strip of land facing **Sutton Road** and extending from **Talbot Street** to the present Talbot Road entrance had not been included in the park. It was feared that unsightly building might take place there so the Corporation purchased the land from **John Brinton** in 1906.

A Grand Opening took place on May 12th 1906. The extension to the park was opened by **Mrs. Tomkinson**. Her husband **Mr. Michael Tomkinson** had been very active in the furtherance of the project.

The fence dividing the newly acquired six and a quarter acres was left in place at that time and it was stated:

> "At present there is no intention to lay out the [new] park in an ornamental manner or to remove the whole of the fence which has divided it from the older parts of the park. Some of the land is being used for instructional gardens, and 16 allotments are under the care of young men who are being trained in the 'proper cultivation of the soil'. A few swings may probably be erected, and the space for the present, devoted to cricket, football and other pastimes for the youth of the borough." [*This would appear to be in the area of the children's playground of today.*]

It continues:

> "For some years, during the summer months, a military band has played selections of music on one evening in the week and it is hoped that adequate support will be given to enable **"Music in the Park"** to be one of the attractions in the summer season."

Original 1896 Bandstand
Kidderminster Reference Library

Mr. Frank Rowley by one of the Crimean canons displayed in the park c1930
Kidderminster Reference Library

At some time before **World War I** two Crimean cannons were placed in the park.
In World War I Kidderminster inhabitants subscribed substantial amounts to war funds.
William Whitcomb, the diarist makes an early mention of a tank being on view in Lion Yard in 1917.

Tomkinson and Hall relate in their book *Kidderminster:*

> "One of the campaigns that were held [in Kidderminster] was a **Tank Week**. It began on Sunday April 14th 1918 and was based on the fund-raising tank named "Julian". Tanks had been introduced on the Western Front only a few months earlier and were objects of great interest. Their use in fundraising had caught the public imagination and the efforts of "Julian" had so far raised £45 million.

Mrs V. Hill, her mother, friend & son in pram, Brinton Park
Courtesy Mrs Hill

The tank was driven down **Comberton Hill** on Sunday afternoon, but broke down whilst negotiating a barrier of sandbags placed opposite **George Street**. Repairs to the track of the tank were necessary and these proved difficult; in fact it was not until Thursday morning that the tank was placed opposite the **Rowland Hill** statue. "Julian" left the town on Saturday. April 20th after a most successful campaign."
[*Tanks were notoriously unreliable at the time.*]

Armistice Day took place on the 11th of November of that year, but 'Peace Day' wasn't celebrated until July 19th of the next year, when the servicemen had returned home and the influenza epidemic had abated. William Whitcomb wrote:

> "We went early to the Park and saw the huge marquees where the soldiers dined, the ox roasting and slicing, and the huge bonfire. We listened to the band and saw the sports. The children had their tea in their respective schools then assembled in the centre of the town by the Town Hall, sang four songs then marched to the Park. Later it rained but we were able to see the bonfires and the fireworks."

Tomkinson and Hall continue:

> ".... the National War Savings Committee presented to the town a 28 ton tank direct from the battlefield. On Saturday August 2nd 1919 a brief handing over ceremony was held at the Rowland Hill statue, after which the tank named "**Emily**" in honour of the **Mayoress Mrs. Ray**, was driven via Exchange Street, New Road. Castle Road and Park Lane into **Brinton Park**, where it was placed on a prepared concrete foundation. Here it remained until **1940** when it was broken up for scrap to aid another war effort." [*Her husband Joseph had been re-elected Mayor in November 1918.*]

There are several photographs of the tank named Emily and the two cannons taken on the high ground by the **Bowling Green** at the **Park Lane** end of the park.

Kidderminster Reference Library

There was a **Cabbies Shelter** in the Park as can be seen in the picture, it was moved there from the Bull Ring, it was shown on a postcard photograph of the 1890's, and would appear to be the one donated by John Brinton to the cabbies. It was used for storing bowls and putting green equipment, but unfortunately was vandalized and was demolished in the late 1990's.

The first Floral Fete was held on August 11th 1928. William Whitcomb remarked:

> "The Flower Show was on the small side but the sports were the most popular part of the Fete."

A new bandstand was officially opened on May 27th 1934 by the **Mayoress Mrs. G. R. Woodward**, (who was a much loved lady) to replace the one built in 1896. The photograph shows the 1935 concert for the GeorgeV Jubilee Celebrations. The stand being appropriately inscribed 'God Save the King.' William Whitcomb attended that celebration in the park. He wrote that after the children had had their tea party and been presented with their mug, they were taken to Brinton Park "where all sorts of

Bandstand - 1935 Jubilee Celebrations
Kidderminster Reference Library

entertainment was provided. Surely the park never had such a crowd in it. Fireworks were begun at 9.45 and the huge bonfire which was erected on old Aggboro' was lighted at 10 'clock. Our decorations are remaining up in the town for a whole week and the buildings are to be floodlit every night."

Both Baldwins' and Kidderminster Bands were in attendance together with 'Mr. Arthur Howley and Concert Party' and Miss Patsy Heath and pupils with a dancing display.

Two years later the park hosted the main Coronation celebration in May 1937 with a similar programme of entertainment.

The new Sons of Rest Pavilion, Brinton Park, Kidderminster
Kidderminster Reference Library

Another photograph shows the new Sons of Rest Pavilion (which replaced the Old Pals Shelter) with Sir **George Eddy** at the opening on the 2 July 1938. Sir George headed the list of donors, many of his friends subscribed to the fund. The pavilion was altered and added to in memory of Harry Bridges in May 1955. The Old Pals Shelter was made into an office for the groundsman with a storeroom for tennis and other equipment. Mr. Duce was the Park Keeper for many years. There was a café in the park at that time.

The **Four Winds Shelter** housed **Mrs. Butcher's 'Little Candy Shop'** much loved by the children. It was there in the 1930s until World War II.

David Gaston gives us some insights into **World War II** activities in the park. Bert French was Park Superintendent during the war. An air-raid shelter was built in the park and a large water tank for the use of the fire services.

The 'Four Winds' shelter - it's vandalised remains were removed in 2004   Kidderminster Reference Library

The **'Holidays at Home'** campaign brought much varied entertainment to the when people were unable to visit the seaside and country, through lack of transport, and the fact that many beaches were mined and barricaded for fear of invasion. **Elsie Dyer**, **Patsy Heath** and **Fay Viner**, dancing teachers, put on dancing shows with their pupils. **Talent Competitions** were popular, amateurs competed for a prize by singing, dancing or even conjuring.

David says that several weeks before **D Day** an American Army Corps of black soldiers took a wrong turn in the black-out with their vehicles, turning left at **Talbot Street** for **Stourport Road**, their lorries having trailers loaded with high explosives, they were unable to turn back, so with headlights beaming (forbidden in war-time) they climbed the bank and drove over into **Stourport Road**. Their progress was marked next morning by the amount of orange peel and banana skins (unobtainable to civilians) that littered the roadway! They often parked their vehicles alongside a hedge on the town side where the children's playground is now.

Roger Mathews remembers climbing the trees with other boys and the irate park keeper waving them down and chasing them with his stick. One of the bushes on the Sutton Road side was the boys 'aeroplane', its shape gave room for wings and places for the pilot and gunner. He joined the crowds that had been drawn there with his mother on VE Day. Great excitement was generated by the grand 'pig roast'; the bandstand vibrated there with music from bands, soloists sang and all kinds of entertainments had been got together for the long awaited occasion.

The extremely cold winters of 1940, 1946/7 and 1963 saw much snowballing and tobogganing in the Park. The steep banks were ideal for the purpose.

For those living in the Sutton Park area at that time, the Park was a regular place to visit, and for people living further afield, it was a visit to prepare for with a picnic in the summer, a long walk and some anticipation.
Brass Bands and Military Brass Bands in the Band Stand were still very popular after the war in the late forties and the fifties. Friends can remember that it was difficult to find a place to sit down on the grass. As well as the advertised programme requests from the audience were played. Band concerts always concluded with "God Save the King" (or Queen) when everybody stood to attention. This was both out of respect for the monarch and as a show of patriotism.

The **1st Festival of Kidderminster** took place in **1969** when crowds of people flocked to the Park.

The Wren's Nest
The Wrens Nest Pub on the Stourport Road edge of the Park was first listed in a Directory in **1879**, this was before the Park was made. At the far end a terraced house adjoined it.

Mr. and Mrs. Smith the first landlords of the Park Inn, with their family.
Courtesy of Linda Bishop

The **Park Inn** on Stourport Road was opened on the 5th of December 1913. Mr. and Mrs Smith were the first landlords. The photograph shows them with their family in the back garden. The Pub still serves the community today.

JOHN BRINTON M. P., J. P. 1827-1914

John Brinton was the son of Henry Brinton, who was a successful carpet and rug manufacturer. John was born on January 25th in a house in Mill Street, Kidderminster, later used by F. C. Broome who was a merchant and manufacturer. His grandfather was William Brinton who was also a manufacturer in the town as early as 1800. William was for many years partner in the firm of Cooper and Brinton, Carpet Manufacturers.

In later years John was proud of the fact that his grandfather had been the first to establish Sunday Schools in Kidderminster. He was Superintendent of Old Meeting Sunday School for many years.

John was born just a year before the **1828 Carpet Weavers Strike**. During one night strikers pelted his fathers' residence in Mill Street with stones and other missiles. Most of the windows were broken. John was sleeping peacefully on a bed in the front room when the stones began to smash the furniture and he was hurriedly taken to a place of safety. It was said that he had received a "Baptism of Fire". As a boy he left home to be educated privately in Birmingham. He was a boarder with eight other pupils at Guildford House, Gower Place, in Wheeler Street. Henry Smith was the Schoolmaster.

At that time his father Henry, a carpet manufacturer, was living at Drayton House, near Belbroughton, while his brother Henry, aged 15 was living in the household of Mr. Henry Moore and his wife Mary, in Lion Street, Kidderminster. Mr. Moore was a bell-hanger.

Henry Brinton senior had started business in 1819 on a site near the Brinton Offices in Exchange Street. John joined the family business in 1842 when he would have been about fifteen, he spent six years as a learner with his brother Henry and was made partner in the firm in 1848. Upon the death of both his father and brother Henry in 1857, he assumed sole charge of the company.

The business was very successful. The firm exhibited at the Great Exhibition of 1851 in London and later at the Paris Exhibition in 1867 when they gained the only Gold Medal for English Carpets.

The 1851 census shows John at 24, unmarried, with his own residence, living next door to his father **Henry** in **Farfield**. (His father's house was later described in a Directory as **Farfield Cottage** and exists today under the name of Farfield House.) His widowed sister Sarah Broome, was living in the house also, with her children, Edward aged 4 and Frank aged 1.

John Brinton appears on that census as a partner with his father and brother in a Carpet Rug making firm employing 145 men, 20 women, 40 boys and 60 girls. By the 1861 census he was living in **Shrubbery House** (Birmingham Road) with his wife Anne (formerly Oldham, who was born in Ireland) and their four children, Margaret 6, Madeline 4, Brenda 2 and Joshua 1 year old, (who appears on the 1871 census as Selwyn John Curwen Brinton), and four servants. Anne died in July 1863.

By 1871 John Brinton had moved to **Moor Hall**, Lower Mitton, Stourport, with his second wife Mary, born in Limerick, Ireland and a new family, John three, Reginald one year and an infant daughter 10 days old. The earlier children are not listed at home on the census, but Brenda a daughter from his first marriage, can be traced to The Bury School in Malvern. The family were employing no less than ten servants. **Moor Hall** was a very extensive property with nine bedrooms. The size of the house was perhaps commensurate with the size of his family and his position as the largest carpet manufacturer in Kidderminster. This was a period when he was in contention with his workers as he tried unsuccessfully to introduce tapestry looms worked by women who were to be paid 40% less than men in wage; a time when change from hand to power working was inevitable.

Moor Hall was only occupied by John Brinton, a male caretaker, a housekeeper and two servants at the time of the 1881 census, probably his wife and some of the children were in London, because by then he had been elected M. P. for Kidderminster and he and the family were dividing their time between London and Stourport. His son Reginald, from his second marriage was at Arden School House at Wooton Wawen, Warwickshire.

His wife Mary suffered from heart disease and found that town life in London didn't suit her, so they returned to Moor Hall with John commuting between there and London. The travelling took a toll on his health, and he very unwillingly agreed to stand for Parliament again, he was re-elected but soon after Mary's condition became worse. She died in February 1887 aged 46 years and was buried in Lower Mitton churchyard next to her son William who had died in November 1872, her eldest daughter Mary had died in 1866. She left behind four sons and two daughters, the youngest child was not yet four years old. The same year John suffered a serious illness and could not be prevailed upon to stand for Parliament again though he was pressed to do so 'in the Liberal interest and as a supporter of Ministerial Policy with regard to Ireland.'

The family were not resident at Moor Hall at the time of the two subsequent censuses in 1891 and 1901. John Brinton is recorded as having travelled extensively in many countries and had business connections abroad, so it is possible that they were travelling or staying elsewhere. In1890 he married a third wife, Mary Jane Gething. A small portrait that the family have, shows that she strongly resembled Queen Alexandra, Mary died in June 1903. John Brinton later, I am told, married his nurse. So though eminently successful in his business and local interests, his life was punctuated by bereavement in his family life. However ten children of the first two marriages survived into adulthood. He was at Moor Hall for his 82nd birthday party in 1909 when it was reported that most of his family were present. He was resident there until his death.

Among many services to the town **John Brinton** granted permission for a bridge to be built by the Corporation over the Stour alongside his works in **1878**. It stretched from Corporation Street to the canal side near the old cemetery. It allowed access over the river from the **Wood Street - Park Street** area and saved workers a long detour to reach their places of work before **Castle Street** was made from the **Caldwell Castle** driveway in **1897**.

He held many chairmanships. As Chairman of the Board of Guardians, a post he held for 14 years, he cast the deciding vote in **1881** to the motion that the present workhouse should be rebuilt on a new site. However this decision was rescinded soon after because of ratepayers alarm at the prospect of increased rates. The existing workhouse was extended with

The Bridge over River Stour near Caldwell Tower
Kidderminster Reference Library

some new buildings, which resulted in the demolition of the **Tap House Inn** (built about 1820 and its acclaimed bowling-alley, the site was later occupied by the Post Graduate Centre that served Kidderminster General Hospital, it has in turn been replaced by the present Treatment Centre. John Brinton was one of the founders of the School of Science and Art (originally known as the School of Design) he was Chairman of the Committee for twenty years and for many years was Chairman of Trustees at the High School for Girls. As Chairman of the Governors of Powick Asylum he took a keen interest in the welfare of the patients and was Chairman there for twenty years. In 1879 he founded the Kidderminster Chamber of Commerce and was its first President.

He had literary and artistic taste and a love of travel and sport. He was active locally in sporting circles, belonging in one period to the Archery Club, and was President of the Harriers Football Club 1881/2. In 1889 he held the office of High Sheriff of Worcestershire. These are but a few of his many offices and interests. Travelling all over the world he wrote and spoke of what he had seen. He was a fellow of the Society of Antiquities and took a warm interest in the archaeology of the county.

John Brinton was also a generous benefactor. Early in **1893** he offered to pay for the restoration of the tower of **St. Mary's Parish Church**. The work was carried out between **1893** and **1895** and cost £7,000. Also at that time the approach to the church was widened and made more attractive. Soon after he became a lay reader and in December **1899**, it was believed, became the first layman ever to preach in the church.

Another benefaction was that of the fountain at Worcester Cross in **1876**. His good works for the town were acknowledged at a ceremony on March 19th **1904** when he became the first **Freeman of Kidderminster**.

In the biographical article in the Kidderminster Shuttle of February 1901 when he celebrated his 82nd birthday, it is reported that John Brinton spoke warmly of Municipal developments and of his sadness at the previous conditions of Artisans 60 and 70 years before, and the miseries endured by the change from old hand to power driven carpet looms. Old rookeries had been swept away and good dwellings for the artisan class had been erected. The town had been well drained and given a splendid water supply. He recalled his Parliamentary contest of 21 years before, when he was struck with the vastly improved sanitary conditions under which families lived compared to a few years prior to 1860. He spoke also of progress in Poor Law provision and said that it was no wonder that the workhouse was feared, and said that: "it had been a mistake not to rebuild the workhouse. It was a cheeseparing operation to patch up and make extensions."

In his Obituary in the Kidderminster Shuttle of the 4th of July 1914 it was recorded that John Brinton 'Took a keen interest in local and general questions,' and that 'His long life of strenuous endeavour was dominated by the highest principles.' Elsewhere it was stated that he did not shy away from confrontation and was of a strong mind.

Most if not all of his ten children appear to have had interesting lives, Selwyn an M.A., was described as a 'distinguished writer and critic' and appears as a solicitor in 1901, while Reginald was a J. P., John Chaytor was a Major in the 2nd Lifeguards and Oswald Walter was a Colonel of the 21st Lancers. In 1891 John Chaytor held the post of Gentleman Usher to the King. Cecil was a director in the firm, Robert Percival was an Anglican priest, and one of John's daughters had been described in 1887 as 'labouring in South Africa in connection with the Church of England Africa Mission'. Reginald took over the Chairmanship of the company upon his father's death and was made Mayor of Kidderminster.

John Brinton's funeral took place at St. Mary's Church, Kidderminster. Work people who wished to join the funeral procession which was starting from Moor Hall, Lower Mitton, were asked to be at the "Stourport Road gate of the Park at 1-30 p.m." A tomb to John Brinton's memory, that of his third wife and of two of his children stands in front of St. Mary's Parish Church. His fourth wife was present at his funeral.

Brinton Park

View of the pool c1904 - Courtesy Kidderminster Reference Library

View towards Park Lane - Courtesy Kidderminster Reference Library

Brinton Park

Richard Eve Monument 2008 - Courtesy Wyre Forest Cultural Services

RICHARD EVE

You may have passed the monument in the park many times and wondered who was **Richard Eve** to deserve so great a monument? Surely it should have been a monument to **John Brinton** who gifted the park to the people of Kidderminster? However John Brinton was very much alive at the time it was built and didn't die until **1914**, so it wouldn't have been a consideration. The fact that he was made the first Freeman of Kidderminster soon after in **1904**, showed the town's appreciation for his many benefactions including the park. It is accepted by those who have researched the records that the monument, as well as being a memorial to Richard Eve, is also an expression of Liberalism, a cause for which Richard Eve was an enthusiastic supporter as well as being a great benefactor of Masonic causes.

He was an example of someone who had succeeded in life far beyond the expecta- tions of the status of the family that he was born into. Liberalism was very strong in Kidderminster at the time and leading Liberal figures in Kidderminster subscribed to the fund. Although he spent such a comparatively short part of his life in Kidderminster, it was a formative period, he remained in touch with his friends there and indeed stood as their Liberal candidate for parliament on two occasions.

The monument itself unveiled on June 15th **1902** is fully worthy of restoration. The Kidderminster Times of June 21st informs us that the drinking fountain was erected to the designs of **Mr. Joseph Pritchard** who was then head of the firm of architects then known as Messrs Meredith & Pritchard.

"The height of the fountain being nearly 30 feet, including the base, is in the Renaissance style, and built of the glazed Doulton ware, which is claimed to be impervious to atmospheric influences and therefore practically imperishable. It has been treated in colours of green, terracotta and golden bronze. The medallion is the work of a sculptor named Mr. Broad, a native of Chaddesley Corbett. The work has been carried out by Messrs. Doulton & Co. of Lambeth. The foundations for the monument were put in by Messrs. George Brown & Sons, Monumental Masons of Coventry Street, Kidderminster."

The cost of the monument, excepting the foundations, was about £500. **Richard Eve** was born in Kidderminster the fourth son and youngest child of **John** and **Ann Eve** on the 6th December 1831 in **Bromsgrove Street**. He was born slightly disabled and suffered some lameness.

His father, who was born in Essex, had come to **Kidderminster** from **Bradford** where his second son **George** was born. His son **John** and a probable sister **Sophia** were born in Lancashire, his wife's birthplace. John could have travelled from Essex by waterway to the north in search of work, because it was a time of high unemployment in Essex and Surrey. There was little work on the land and his trade of woolcomber in Essex was one that could be expected to find him employment in one of the northern wool towns. It would appear that he was not satisfied there and Richard Eve's obituary states that his father came to Kidderminster to take up the post of foreman in the Spinning Department at **Hooman and Pardoe's** Works.

Richard Eve's brothers were **John, George** and **Benjamin**. He attended **Pearsall's Grammar School**: one of the schools on the **New Meeting Unitarian Chapel** site in **Church Street** that was eventually amalgamated with New Meeting Schools. The Grammar School had been established in order to prepare boys for the ministry of the Unitarian Church.

At the time of the census of **1841** the family were living at **Spring Bank, Leswell**, (by the **1851** census it was called **Leswell Bank**). Richard's father was then described as a 'Woolcomber Journeyman'. They were living near to **Leswell Cottage** (the large Georgian house that still stands there), Richard was 10 at that time. None of the boys are listed as having any employment, though they were 15, 13, 11 and 10, so perhaps they were also at school with Richard or at nearby **St. George's School**, it had opened in 1827. If that were so it would mark them out as a family with aspirations. Also it was quite likely that **Richard's** association with the **Unitarians**, who were very actively engaged in educating the poor as well as other social enterprises, influenced his character and bore fruit in his later life when he became prosperous. His early experiences in Kidderminster must have been important to him for he kept in touch with his friends there and often visited his birthplace.

On leaving school **Richard** worked at the offices of **Henry Talbot** collecting rents. A **Sophia Eve** aged 15 was listed on the census as a female servant in **Oaklands House** the home of **Henry and Ann Talbot** in 1841, and was most probably Richard's sister since there are no other families of that name in Kidderminster on the 1841 census and she was shown as being born outside the county. At 15 years of age Richard was articled to Mr. **A .S. Field**, Solicitor, of **Leamington**.

In **1851** the Census shows Richard aged 19 years lodging in the **High Street** at **Leamington Priors** in the house of an architect; Edmund Mitchell. **Richard** was described then as a 'Solicitor's writing clerk'. It was while he was in Leamington that he joined Guy's [Masonic] Lodge and was elected Master in **1855**.

Richard's family were still in **Kidderminster** in **1851** living at **Leswell Bank**, his father's occupation was now described as an 'accountant' while his brother **John** 24, was a woolcomber, **George** 22, a 'Taylor Master' and **Benjamin** 21, a woolstapler. **Sophia** cannot be traced in the census, she would probably have married by then and consequently changed her surname.

In **1861** only **Richard** was at the home of his parents, which was now in a cottage at the rear of Kings Road, Chelsea. His father had changed his occupation again and was now described on the census as 'Fancy Soap Manufacturer', he could perhaps also have been described as an entrepreneur! **Richard** 29 was listed as 'Legal Profession'. He may have been visiting his parents, for in **1862** he was elected Master of the Brecon Lodge of Freemasons. In **1863** he joined the Panmure Lodge in **Aldershot,** this would appear to be the year that he went there to live.

The Aldershot News writes in his obituary: "he arrived in the town with no prospects other than those which his own industry should give out for him, it is said that when he took possession of a tiny office and boldly put up the notice in the window '**Richard Eve Solicitor**' he had scarcely the wherewithal to furnish the place except in the most modest fashion".

Aldershot at that time was undergoing great change, the Army wanted to build a large permanent camp for the training of troops on a large scale. The area around Aldershot was thought to be particularly suitable both for its position, and the large areas of infertile heath land that surrounded it. It was growing from being an insignificant village into a town that would be known worldwide as the 'Home of the British Army'.

Soon after he arrived in Aldershot, Richard was appointed as Vestry Clerk and Clerk of the Burial Board and was shortly elected Chairman of the Urban District Council. He also served on the Hampshire County Council. In **1870** he was elected Worshipful Master of the Freemasonry Lodge. He had a number of Freemasonry appointments, including for many years the Chairmanship of the Board of Management of the Masonic Boy's school. He eventually became a member of the Grand Master's Lodge, the Grand Master being the Prince of Wales at the time of Eve's death. The Prince wrote at the time of his last illness expressing sympathy and the wish that he would be spared.

He was described in the **1871** census as 'Solicitor', living in **Victoria Road** (a road of detached villa's) with **Maria Browning** as his 59 years old General Servant. He would appear to have improved his situation in a very short time. Described as 'Solicitor & Notary', he was still in **Victoria Road** in **1881** still supported by a housekeeper and a general servant.'

It was in **1885** that Richard Eve first stood for Parliament: in the Basingstoke division of Hampshire. He contested seats twice in **1886**, and then again in**1887**, all unsuccessfully. Then in **1890** he had already been selected to contest St. George's ward in East London, when he was approached to come to **Kidderminster** to address the Liberal membership, he sacrificed that opportunity in favour of Tony Benn's grandfather, who went on to win the seat for the Radical interest.

He spoke on "Law and Order" at the Town Hall in Kidderminster, dealing with the Irish question. After which he was invited to stand as candidate for the borough as a champion for Liberalism. The election took place in July **1892**, he did not succeed, **Frederick Godson** gained 2,066 votes and **Richard Eve** 1,801. When he contested a further election in Kidderminster in **1895** not many people had changed sides for the results then were **Godson** 2,008; **Eve** 1,713.

Richard Eve was a member of the National Liberal Club in London, where he would have stayed on business trips.

During the time of these events he had moved house. In **1891** he was in **Station Road,** where he had built four houses, his address was now **2 Devereux Houses**, Station Road where he lived with just the help of a 25 years old housekeeper. At number one lived 40 years old **Charles Bateman** described as a Solicitor's Managing Clerk, no doubt in the employ of **Richard** and his partner **Norman Clinton**. Mr. Clinton continued in the practise after the death of Richard Eve.

Richard Eve was still fulfilling his many engagements immediately before his death although he had caught a chill early in May and had been ordered to bed. He subsequently had a seizure of cerebral haemorrhage. His death on July 7th 1900 took place at the London Nursing Institute where he had been cared for during the last two weeks of his life.

The funeral took place in Aldershot, the service being conducted by the Rev. E. D. Priestley Evans of the New Meeting House at Kidderminster.

He left £500 to the New Meeting Chapel. He was said to have intended to present Greenhill House with 14 acres of grounds, to the people of Kidderminster, but died before this was accomplished.

Richard Eve Monument c 1902
Kidderminster Reference Library

SUTTON COMMON AREA BEFORE BRINTON PARK

The development of the Sutton Common area and the tales of life there before the Park was gifted to the town is examined through the writings of **Ebenezer Guest**, a local historian, who lived in Kidderminster from his birth in 1822 until his death in 1913. He was a very valuable local historian whose memories of life in Kidderminster in the 19th century were published as a series of articles in the *Kidderminster Shuttle* in from 1906 -1908. It is well to keep in mind that he was writing one hundred years ago about places as they were, and events that had happened often fifty or more years before he wrote! These extracts as written give the feel of the times. His articles were first of all about the Horsefair area that he lived in, but they were so popular that he extended his articles to contain reminiscences of other parts of the town.

Sutton or **Suduuale** was mentioned in the Domesday Book as one of the 16 outliers of Kidderminster. No doubt it continued as farm or common land until the Industrial Revolution when it began to be urbanised in response for the need for housing for successful industrialists, more particularly carpet manufacturers and their workers.

Development on the Sutton side of the town was slow because of the barrier of the Redstone cliff known as **Mount Skipet**. It would seem that the earliest development there was that of **Carpet Hall** (later known as Carpet Hill), followed by the development of **Hill Street**, **Brussels Street** and **Park Street** to house the workers, while successful business men including Carpet manufacturers built houses on **Bewdley Hill** and in the **Blakebrook area**.

Mount Skipet - the original two cottages that were part of the first carpet premises of John Pearsall 1735   Courtesy of David Jones

The men who lived in the former streets and worked in **Carpet Hall** were mostly described as 'Hand Loom Weavers', and the women and girls as "Worsted Factory Hands" on the 1851 census. Draw-boys were employed to separate the threaded frames for the bobbin to travel through, bigger girls sometimes worked as "draw-girls" on the lighter Jacquard frames.

Louisa Carter
When Louisa was aged 13, she was working at Barber and Cole's mill in Church Street, and was one of the 'draw-girls' who was interviewed by Mr. Scriven, the Government Inspector for the Children's Employment Commission in **1842**. He was enquiring into the working hours and conditions of children in the carpet industry.

She lived in **Hill Street** with her widowed mother in **1841**, and was by her own account, having a very poor life then. She told Mr. Scriven that she had worked in the factory since she was ten, she could read but not write although she had gone to day school for two years. Her father, a weaver, was dead and four of the eight children were still at home, three were working. She went to work at six o'clock in the morning and came home about nine in the evening.

When asked about her treatment at work she said: "The men behave middling to us; they never beat us but William Crane sometimes jaws me, and swears at me, and wishes me in Hell; that is when I am not in time for work or am not quick; he is not a steady man, he gets tipsy sometimes; he is not regular at his work; last Wednesday and Thursday he never came nigh the shop; he was out drinking I saw him Thursday night quite drunk. I had to stay at the shop all day until it got dark at night, and then went home without doing any work."

She went on to explain that she had worked "twelve and twelve" [a system that allowed a double shift and was put in force by the manufacturer for rush orders] for three months when the ice and snow were on the ground, in fact she worked from one a.m. to four p.m. the next day fettling the frames and winding the quills, and was, not surprisingly "always very tired" and did not like the night-work.

However ten years later she was married to **Robert Stannard.** They lived in the same house in **Hill Street** with her mother in 1851, later the Stannards moved to **38 Wood Street** and finished their married life in **87 Peel Street**, having taken advantage of the newer houses nearby. There is no evidence to suggest that Louisa worked in the carpet industry again. In **1891** they had a lodger, **Charles J. Dredge**, he took over the house when Robert was widowed in 1896, and by **1901** he had turned it into a grocery and beer shop. Robert then lived next door at number **88** as a lodger. He died in 1903. In more than 60 years the family had stayed near to Louisa's early home, no doubt feeling part of the close local community. *(Kidderminster Reference Library has an interesting essay written by W. H. Edwards entitled "Wood Street around 1918 to 1938" available for loan.)*

Continuing the history of the area

We are able to revisit happenings in the Sutton Common area prior to the opening of the park through the writings of Ebenezer Guest. He wrote:

> "At the end of **Brussels-street** the cliff used to be dangerous and exposed, and on a vacant space behind the **Forge**, in **Park Lane**, a lad was killed by slipping down while gathering blackberries, and the descent was very steep and tiresome to the females employees at **Hill-street** and **Brussels-street**, but through the active and persistent motion of the late Mr. **Alfred Greaves** the dangerous cliff has been walled off and a broad and convenient set of steps have supplied a long and much needed want. Mr. **William Horsfall** was also able to persuade the Corporation to strengthen and raise the wall, and secure the passage from **Hill-street** to the end of **Park-street**, which was in a dangerous state. A walk down **Brussel-street** and round the **Rock Terrace** would well repay anyone who would take it.

'Carpet Steps'
Courtesy Miss M Robinson

The abrupt change of view in a few yards from the crowded town to the **Stour Meadows** and the **Wolverley Church**, cannot be equalled in this locality."

Rock Terrace with Park Butts below
Wyre Forest Museum Services

Richard Dadford outside his wife's (Mary) shop, with daughter Betty 1923
Wyre Forest Museum Services

Sutton Common and the Freehold Land Society

> "The left-hand side of **Sutton Common** was opened by the **Freehold Land Society** about fifty years ago. They purchased the land from Mr. **Henry Talbot** that reached from four cottages (now standing by the old Pound) to the footpath that leads from **Park Lane** to the **Common**. They laid in it out in 93 lots, fenced and fitted it with rustic gates, made a long street from north to south, which they called **Franchise-street**, as one of their objects was to get freehold votes. Three shorter streets were also made, which they named **Hume-street** after **Joseph Hume**, the great economist; **Holman-street** after a local worthy; and **Talbot-street** after the well-known Liberal family.

[Freehold land societies had come into existence in the 1840s following the Reform Act of 1832. The most important voting qualifications then, were the ownership of a freehold with a minimum value of 40 shillings, and the occupation of a house worth at least £10 a year. The housing developments in the Sutton Common area provided Kidderminster with much needed improved accommodation for its' artisans.]

> **George Law** was called in to remove a sand hill and disperse the contents where needed. The first house built was opened as a beer-house, and the landlord gave an excellent housewarming where political speeches and sentiments were the order of the evening, and much enthusiasm was shown.

> **Hume-street** has since become the site of an excellent **Board School**; another land society has joined up to the first, and **Franchise-street** has been extended into **Bewdley-street**. On the other, or foreign side of the **Common** they bought six houses in **Washington Row**. This and all the other purchases by the kindred societies have been successes and largely helped to shape the growth of the town."

Park Butts and Park Lane

The Horn and Trumpet Public House shouldn't go without mention for Ebenezer gives a detailed and atmospheric description of life and happenings in that Pub in the mid-19th century. It is first mentioned in a Directory in 1820, but is probably older than that. The building still survives today. He writes:

> "No description of **Park-lane** in the old days can be complete without a notice of **William Clewes** and the **Horn and Trumpet**…. He was a red faced, full sized, broad shouldered man, with a cheery expression and a rough humour of his own, and had a knowledge of all the faults and failings of his customers, who often told him slyly of incidents which he would polish up and use on a future occasion. His beer was excellent, and he saw everyone served promptly, and knew all his customers specialities, and needed no telling twice. He had an excellent memory.

> Every night his parlour bar was full, and whist was the game. When there were twelve players others must wait, and the humblest had his turn. They paid fourpen'orths (1s. 4d. each game), and no-one was allowed to pay until

the company broke up, or a players retired, when Clews would tell each
one what he had to pay, and he was always right. Sometimes some one
would contradict or in some way offend him, when he would begin to
mutter observations as to the offenders dress, accent, gait any peculiarity,
amid the titters and guffaws of the company…. Nobody was offended or
else they did not come again until at last it was understood there would be
a passage at arms, and there would be a crowded house. Many well to do
frolicsome men were there, who said they came to hear "Old Billy".

(This story is reminiscent of the small clubs that assembled in such Public Houses in both the
18th and 19th centuries.)

Removing the Cliff

"Before the work of removing the great cliff and making it possible to get
up what is now called **Bewdley-street**, this [**Park Lane**] was the road to
Bewdley."

Apparently the way to Bewdley was along Park Lane, up the bank, along what became Talbot
Street, over Sutton Road to the Great Field, up through that to the Lea Bank (the 1859 map
shows a diagonal footpath), it then appeared to join what is the present road to Bewdley.

Ebenezer Guest continues:

"**Wm. Butler Best** had an office next to **Mill-street** and carried on a
business as a yarn agent. --- The **Canal** was then much more important
and flourishing than now, and the large space from the **Butts** was called
the **Canal Wharf** and was a very busy place. ---There was a large garden
with a high wall in **Park-lane**. There were some Mulberry trees and fine
old fruit trees in the garden. ---

There was a bath then on the right-hand side of **Park-lane** supplied by a
natural spring; the water ran from it into the lane. A few tradesmen used it,
generally in the morning. There were scarcely a dozen of them and they
were very exclusive.

Shop on the corner of Park Lane before Brinton's Castle Road
Factory was built.   Kidderminster Reference Library

About a year before the [carpet
weaver's] strike Mr. **Frederick
Talbot** had built twenty-four
houses at **Cemetery Row**. Had
he known what was coming he
would have delayed the business.
Mr. **Edward Broadfield** and
myself took them on lease, as
Mr. **Talbot** was leaving the
town. We had one good month
then came the deluge. We
dropped the rents a shilling a
week, but soon had eighteen to twenty vacant."

"The **Castle** was then occupied by an eccentric man named **Hancox**. He fancied he was a poet and used to recite doggerel lines to his customers. It was the last house in the town in that direction and had a large orchard garden. —Sometimes he was induced to go to the **Black Horse** and recite verses upon the news of the day. Such fun!"

Mount Skippet Passage

"Before **Mount Skippett** was pierced through, and a large part of it carted away, the only approach to the upper part of **Blakebrook** end was through the narrow passage by **Goodwin's** cottages, on to **Cussfield**, and the **Old Square**. I have heard my mother say that she carried me in her arms from **Rock Terrace** to the **Olive Tree and Dove**, and I recollect seeing the masons building the wall in front of the

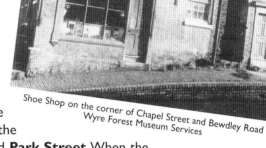

Shoe Shop on the corner of Chapel Street and Bewdley Road Wyre Forest Museum Services

houses between **Chapel Street** and **Park Street**. When the rock had been removed there were a few houses left with a very narrow pathway in front. They were called the **Battery**, but became unsafe and disappeared. So has the **Old Square**."
[*The Old Olive tree and Dove at 88 Bewdley Street, was first mentioned in a Directory in 1840, it closed in 1912.*]

Paying the Lord

"A few small proprietors used to meet at the **Olive Tree** once a year to pay some small acknowledgements to the Lord of the Manor.... But the custom has ceased. There were a few caves in the rock, mostly used by chimney sweeps, and a recess in the rock with a pump, whose water was much prized.

Behind the **Olive Tree** was old **Cussfield,** a few rambling old houses whose roofs used to percolate into the roof of the lower tier that faced what is now **Bewdley Street**. Then came the **Barley Mow**…" [*First mentioned in a Directory in 1793*].

The Old Square

"Then came the **Old Square**, a good-sized well-formed square with cross roads through it and gardens, and a large well. In the inside were some hand-loom shops. One was turned into a Sunday School and supported by the **"Old Meeting."** Mr. **William Brinton**, grandfather of Mr. **John Brinton**, was the superintendent....

There was a public house called the **Nag's Head** [*closed before* 1890] in the square, the **Chartist Headquarters**, and by many supposed to be a complete Chartist Armoury.

The Square reached from the **Barley Mow** to the Grammar School. One part of it now is **Paternoster-row**, and another **Crowther-street**."

Old Square Boxers

"Many of the Old Square lads were sturdy boxers [they] were a terror to **Bewdley** boys who came into town, and sometimes made raids as far as **Churchfields** before they could reach their match."

Open privies

L. D. Smith, in his book Carpet Weavers and Carpet Masters, writes of the terrible sanitary conditions in the town in the mid 19th century when a methodical survey was made of the working class streets. Cussfield, The Battery and the Square in Bewdley Road were among those singled out for particular mention having "open privies, heaps of filth, muck-holes full, and a well between two muck holes". The conditions were a frequent cause of fever. He says that during 1849 large scale cleaning operations were undertaken. Paupers were employed in white-washing, scraping gutters, clearing drains, and removing tons of refuse from courts and alleys. Fire hoses were directed at houses on The Rock, and in the Battery and Blackwell Street.

Sunday Wakes

He also describes the Sunday wakes that took place in the villages around Kidderminster in July and August when such places as "Franche, Hoobrook, Broadwaters and Blakebrook offered amusements of a "very primitive character", and games such as "eating hot rolls and treacle, dancing for pumps, climbing the greasy pole for a leg of mutton", and so on. There might also be bull-baiting, badger drawing, dog fighting and similar sports."

Woodfield House

Woodfield House 1990   Courtesy of Kidderminster Times

"The **Greenhill Farm** was exchanged for **Woodfield House**, and a sum of money given which built the present **Grammar School**. **Woodfield House** became the residence of the Headmaster, the **Rev. W Cockin**, who took in a good many boarders, some of them very well to do. The day scholars were called the town boys, and there was a great deal of ill feeling which came to a head when he declined to take some tradesman's sons as boarders as they were not fit associates for his aristocratic boarders.

This brought matters to a head. Mr. **George Griffith**, corn dealer, afterwards of **Bewdley** took the matter up, and wrote a deal on the subject. Great excitement prevailed. There was a mass meeting in the Market Hall".

The leading men of the town addressed the meeting. A great trial followed in London in which the town tried to prevent the Headmaster having strangers for boarders. The Town lost, the plaintiffs having to pay £100 each, but resulted, writes Ebenezer, in a 'much improved' scheme.

Woodfield House was built in the late 18th century and occupied by James Scawen until his death. An advertisement in Berrow's Journal describes the elaborate furnishings.

To be Sold by Auction
By Samuel Wright

On the 14/15/16 April 1800. General and elegant HOUSEHOLD FURNITURE. POST Chariot with Plated Harness, a Microscope, Quadrant, Reflecting Telescope, Measuring Wheel by Dolland, an Herbarium, mangle and other effects belonging to the late James Scawen of Woodfield House in the Borough of kiddeerminster. Furniture comprises:- Mahogany bedsteads with chintz and cotton furnishings, prime beds and bedding, library book cases, dining, card, Pembroke, writing and side board tables, mahogany and other chairs, an excellent suite of drawing room furniture, large pier glasses, a valuable timepiece with chimes by Delander and an 8 day clock in Mahogany case by Allen and Clements with various other effects to be viewed on the 11th.
Catalogues at the Auctioneers and principal Inns in Kidderminster, Worcester, Stourbridge and Bewdley &c 7 days preceeding sale.

The house was sold to John Cooper a clothier the same year. It was in 1843 that Rev. William Cockin bought the house. The school was at that time housed in the Chantry of St. Mary's Parish Church, Mr. Cockin had a master's house at the top of Church street. As Ebenezer implies the house was too small for his designs. Another consideration was the fact that the Chantry was in a dilapidated condition. A dining room was added to Woodfield House for the boarders. Mr. Cockin also campaigned with Feoffes and others wishing to advance education, to provide money for a new school adjacent to the house.

The New Grammar School Building

The school was built in 15th 16th century style and was superior to the Chantry accommodation. Announcing the opening of the school on June 28th 1848 the Ten Towns Messenger described the building:

"The walls are built of Trimpley stone.... the mellow colour of which presents a pleasing contrast with the dressings which are of Elmley stone."

Kidderminster Grammar School, Bewdley Road
Kidderminster Reference Library

The Worcester Chronicle reported:

"The high old wall that runs in front of Woodfield Row is partly pulled down and will be replaced by ornamental gates and railings, the whole forming a handsome addition to the town."

Don Gilbert, in his book *King Charles Grammar School,* suggests that although we do not know who the architect was, that it was possible to have been Harvey Eginton, who was employed in 1847 by Lord Ward in building a new chancel aisle in the Parish Church; he was paying for both works."

As well as the Chantry being dilapidated, the only playground for the boys was the churchyard, which was detrimental to the tombs and gravestones and possibly to the health of the boys. However a description of the interior of the new building suggests that it was intended for use in the same way as the Chantry had been, with a large hall for all the boys, rather than classrooms. The Headmaster had a private room in the Tower over the entrance.

The school was in use with the necessary additional buildings added over the years, until 1977 when reorganization caused the school to be amalgamated with the Girl's High school on the Chester Road site and become a Comprehensive School under the King Charles 1ˢᵗ name. The former building, now used as a Registry Office provides a historical look to the background for Civil Wedding photographs.

A Roman Catholic Chapel

> "The Roman Catholics had a chapel, which has given its name to a street, and when they removed to **Leswell** it came into the hands of Mr. **John Woodward** then of **Summerhill**, and was used as a nursery for **St. John's Church**.

[*The chapel was reputedly formerly a Methodist Chapel, but no records remain. It was only used by the Catholics between 1831-1834. Subsequently used for school and other purposes, it later became a brewhouse for the nearby Sportsman Public House.*]

> **The Lady Huntingdon's** connexion, considering the old **Ebenezer** chapel [in Horsefair] too near the dwelling houses round it, decided to have one in **Park Street**, neat and commodious; but the congregation were not crowded when I paid them a visit."

The area had been poorly provided with nonconformist meeting places before that time.

St. John's Church

Ebenezer recalls:

> "Building went on so fast [in the area] that it was thought it was high time to have another church. Some handsome sums were subscribed and with the energy of **Vicar Claughton** and the support of **Lord Ward's** family **St. John's** was built and consecrated by Bishop Pepys.

All the church schoolchildren had a procession round the town and had tea in the **Market Hall**. During its first sixty years of life it had only three incumbents."

The Rev. J R. Burton writes in his 'History of Kidderminster' in 1890,

> "One of Dr. Claughton's plans for adapting Church work to modern times was the division of the old town Parish into three districts independent of each other, but all looking to the Vicar of Kidderminster as their Patron. The cost of such a large building was only £4,000 and it is hardly to be expected that it could be a very solid structure, in fact it is not weatherproof, but during its 50 years existence it has welded together its parishioners."

He describes one of the windows commemorating the church's chief benefactor, it was inscribed thus:

> "John Woodward Esq. by whose pious aid this church was in part built and the adjoining schools."

John Woodward was a Carpet Manufacturer, he died as the church was being completed, on April 7ᵗʰ 1838.

The church was built during the years **1837-8** by Henry Herring, a local builder, for a cost of £4,500 and was known as the 'black church' because of the colour of the bricks. It had seats for 1,250 people. It was an early victim of vandalism when coins placed under the foundation stone were stolen.

St. John's Church was extensively extended later in the 1880's. The early photograph shows it before the extensions and the subsequent building of Brook Street alongside, where the Girl's School was built. A formal history of the church has not been found, but the history of the church school below shows much light on the work and activities of the church. The school children attended services there and were taught in school by a succession of Vicars and Curates.

St. John's Church 1880s before alterations

Kidderminster Reference Library

St. John's Church in 1910   Kidderminster Reference Library

Fund raising would have been an ongoing task, as the increasing needs of the three departments, not sufficiently covered by the Diocesan funding, were constantly brought to the Managers by the ever assiduous H. M. Is. However they often gave praise for the good ethos of the schools. Mentions are made of church socials and sports that the children were included in. The inspectors often mentioned good ladies from the church who helped in the girls' school with reading and sewing needs. The church also supported a large Sunday school, it is described as 'Endowed' in the 1841 Government Report to the Commissioners Employment of Children, the school already had 180 pupils and 14 teachers, while the Endowed Day School had 75 pupils and 2 teachers at that time.

In the 20th century the church became known for its' social care and outreach work. When the housing Estate was built at Habberley in the 1960s, the church built the Church Hall there, manned by volunteers. Social activities were provided. The Red Cross used it as their base for organising the Annual Holiday's for poor children, and Christmas shopping trips for the handicapped. Some will remember that one of the project's the church undertook was the distribution of joints from the 'meat mountain' to those in need, in the latter part of the century.

Radical meetings

Just up the road from where St. Johns' Church came to be built, the green was often used as a meeting place for **Chartist**s and rival political parties, there having been much unrest before and after the prolonged **Carpet Weaver's Strike** of 1828. We are grateful to Ebenezer again for the details of one such event.

A riotous election

"The open place in front of **Summer Place**, before the trees were planted   ....was used for many purposes. The strike leaders held their meetings there. Stones were broken and stored there, and in an unlucky day **Mr. Joseph Kitely**, who was then Mayor, thought it would be a very suitable place for an election. This election was a rather remarkable one. Mr. **Robert Lowe's** brilliant talents and moderate views had so commended him to both parties that in 1855 he had been re-elected without any opposition, and when   appointed to office in 1857 it would have been the same but for the action of Mr. **Wm. Boycott**, solicitor of this town. The weavers were suffering from the effects of a disastrous strike. Mr. **Boycott** had ingratiated himself with them, had been liberal personally, to many of them, and had always pleaded their cause. His friends raised the cry of a townsman, and he was proposed.

The only manufacturer who voted for **Boycott** was the late **Edward Hughes** and the cry went round that the manufacturers were all against him. Personal indignities were offered to Mr. **Henry Brinton**, who was then unwell. *[He died the same year.]* Just as the friends of Mr. **Lowe** were preparing for a procession after the declaration of the poll the broken stones began to fly.

One of the first to be struck on the brow, followed by a stream of blood was a leading Conservative Mr. **G. Ferrer Green**. A doctor, who was baiting at the **Tap House**, was unhorsed and knocked about. He was a **Cleobury** man and knew nothing of the election. .... The procession marched rapidly away. A few policemen in the narrow part of the road tried to hold the mob back. One of their number, **John Jukes**, was so injured that in a few days he died from the effects. **Lowe** and his friends, who were being pelted, tried to get up the steps between the church and **Woodfield**, but the steps were filled with people, many of them young, all armed with stones. We had to turn and run on the causeway, which was raised above the highway, and tried to get into **Dr. Sheppard's** grounds by the gate, but he had locked it fearing a row. I ran along the wall and found that the door to the back of the house was unfastened and got them to get in there.

Mr. Lowe's hat had been cut with a stone, and his hair being the colour of silver and being covered with blood looked very serious. **Lowe, James Minifie, James Pardoe, Richard Holman**, myself, and three others got in, and the doors were shut behind us, while the crowd made after **Mr. Broom** and ransacked the **Prince Albert**.

It was a nasty affair, and might have been worse. It shows that the bulk of the Conservative Party did not oppose **Lowe**, as in two years they polled 61 more for **Huddlestone** than for him, and **Lowe** polled more than **Bristow** who had united the Liberal Party."

Ebenezer makes mention of the Tap House. He writes:

> There was no **Union Workhouse** then. The **Woodfield Farm** stretched up to **Sutton-road**, with the exception of the **Tap House**, which was then quite out of town, and a very popular resort for tradesmen. There was a very well arranged bowling alley, commodious seats and sturdy banks. Mr. **Benjamin Kimberley** had the management. **Old Tap House Alley** was I think the prettiest one in Kidderminster, surrounded by gardens and the **Blakebrook** rippling near it with ample seating room round the frame for the spectators."

Tap House Inn - demolished 1889 for Workhouse
extensions   Kidderminster Reference Library

The **Prince Albert** is a familiar public house today on the Bewdley Road. It was built in 1851 and is now a Grade II listed building. **Mrs. Camelia Rowe** the landlady, said that **Prince Albert** came to visit Kidderminster to see the carpet that had been made at Brintons Carpet Factory for Covent Garden, the name of the Pub commemorates his visit.

The Cemetery 1844   Kidderminster Reference Library

The Cemetery

From time immemorial Kidderminster inhabitants had been buried in the churchyard at **St. Mary's Church**. When the non-conformist churches were built, they didn't provide burial ground. The building of **St. George's Church** in 1825, and **St. John's** in 1838 provided two more churchyards. **Roman Catholic's** were meeting in the little chapel in **Chapel Street** before they built the church on the **Birmingham Road** in 1834, but presumably neither had burial space around. So there was no designated space for **Roman Catholic's** and non-conformists in Kidderminster before the **Cemetery** was provided.

Ebenezer Guest explains how the cemetery came about:

> "When the **Rev. Richard Fry** [of **New Meeting**] died, and there was an objection to his burial at the **Old Church** [St. Mary's], the **Nonconformists** of Kidderminster, who formed a wealthy and important body, felt it a rather humiliating position to be in, not to have a place of their own to bury without reference to or favour from any one, and largely with Mr. **Turton's** help, they formed a company and bought the site of the present **Old Cemetery** and equipped it with a handsome and suitable chapel and caretaker's house. Later on the town authorities saw the benefit such a possession would be to the town, bought out the old company and largely added to its area, and laid it out in **Episcopal** and **Roman Catholic** portions, the Non- conformists retaining their old ground, and acquiring some new on the south and south-west sides."

Scott Pettitt has told me a story related by his grandmother concerning a local eccentric named **William Wood** who achieved considerable notoriety in the 1920's. He was a native of Highley. On his return from the United States he made his final home in a bungalow in Hemming Street named 'White House' (built in 1927). It can still be identified for it has a tablet inscribed with its name and date. In the book 'Characters of Kidderminster' Mr. Joe Perrin recalled him: "Another character was Mr. Wood, he went out to the U.S.A. and came back having made good. At the top of Kidderminster he had himself built a granite and marble vault ready for when he died, a big, big job with a pinnacle on top, steps down to it and a slab inside, when it was finished he laid himself down on the slab to make sure it would fit him!" He died in 1929 at the age of 80 and lies buried under the enormous granite obelisk at the very top on the Municipal Cemetery, just inside the Holman Street entrance.

Ebenezer describes here a walk that we can't accomplish today. Contemporary maps show the pool to have been a large one.

The Walk by Lodge Pool

"One of the prettiest walks in the town used to be over and on the **Woodfield** farm, now entirely absorbed. Part of the barn remains opposite **Woodfield** house, in **Bewdley-Street**.

The walk began on **Sutton Common** near the **Old Pound**, kept by **Allan Brooks**, and seldom without some hungry looking tenants, and went on to **Park Lane**. There was a large pool, called the **Lodge Pool**, in the upper part of the valley, formed by the pounding up of the **Blakebrook**, and on the dam was a picturesque looking house.

At one time an Oxford boat builder rented the house and had some boats out for hire, and built racing boats for some of the neighbouring gentry. The pool was largely used, and being of varying and uncertain depth was the scene of many tragedies. Two brothers were drowned in trying to save the life of a friend….

There was a beautiful walk on either side of the pool when there were new trees growing or the hawthorn in bloom it was a great treat to see them. At one time this was the way from **Caldwell** to **Bewdley**…."

The New Housing
Woodfield Estate
It can be seen that Ebenezer Guest regarded **Wood Street** as being the central and most important of the new streets that had been built -

Woodfield Crescent Coronation Party 1953
Wyre Forest Museum Services

"some by the **Freehold Land Society** and some by the more pretentious **Woodfield Estate of** which Mr. **Robert Wilkinson** was secretary. It opened out **Cobden Street**, and the **Woodfield Crescent** to the **Cemetery. Councillor Henry Bennet** engineered **Peel** and **Plimsoll-streets**; and Mr. **Councillor Perks** and a few others extended **Park Street** to the **Cemetery.** The societies were all successful and the streets are all broad and cheerful, the houses of a superior kind. - Five out-door licenses and two public houses were built: the **Sportsman** [25 Wood Street] and the **Unity** in Park Street."

"The **Unity** supplies a great public want, and was the subject of much opposition. The inhabitants were nearly unanimous in asking for it: even teetotallers coming forward to speak for the license as a great public accommodation." Both of the latter mentioned pubs still serve the public today.

Wood Street

"Of the nest of new streets that so largely constitute the **Park Ward**, **Wood-street** is the central and most important, some of the older ones were built   upon land purchased from Mr. **Matthew Jeffries**, of **Blakebrook House**, and cover a belt reaching from **Bewdley-street** to a line level with the far end of **Chapel-street**. **Wood-street** when I knew it first stopped at this level with the back walls of Chapel Court. Then the **Freehold Land Society**, held at Mr. **Batham's**, **Church-street**, bought a strip of land, 40 yards deep, reaching to the **Cemetery** wall, and a smaller plot under the **Cemetery** wall from Mr. **Henry Talbot**, who took down the hedge then growing across it and gave the street all the way, reserving the left or eastern side for himself. Mr. **Charles Hargraves** bought a piece on the left hand and built the **Sportsman** [in 1857], which he kept for many years and was followed by Mr. John Webb…."

Woodfield Street

The **Woodfield Tavern** was called "the Lads House", and had a wooden elephant for the use of its youthful customers. Mary Westwood who started her teaching career as a Pupil Teacher at St. John's Girls' School lived there in 1861, with her father Henry, her mother Maria and four brothers and sisters.

The Union Workhouse
Ebenezer writes:

"Then there was the building of the **Bastille** as the new **Union Workhouse** was called. Angry men visited the place speculating on its use and the need for it. If one leader had come to the front a riot might have been organized. Hundreds of people visited it daily to revile its promoters and foretell the ruin which they would bring on Kidderminster to all concerned."

The **Workhouse** was built in 1837-8 and was known as **No.1 Sutton Road** or **"The Grubber"**. It was built as a result of he Poor Law Act of 1834, it demanded that unions of local workhouses such as Kidderminster, Bewdley and Stourport were made resulting in the Kidderminster Union. Those people in need were discouraged from seeking Parish Relief by the threat of being put in the workhouse. It was considered a disgrace.

Overcrowding
By **1870** there were 280 inmates, increasing to 323 by 1881. This number was causing serious overcrowding. After much discussion a brewery, boiler house, bakery, laundry and washhouse, children's quarters and Infirmary buildings for both sexes were added and the former infectious hospital was converted into an infirmary for helpless cases. There were very few able-bodied people seeking admittance most were old and past working age, or children orphaned or abandoned by their parents. After its closure a part of it was used as a geriatric hospital.

In **1947** it was renamed **Blakebrook County Hospital**, later renamed **Kidderminster General Hospital** and recently been renamed **Kidderminster Treatment Centre**.

Mrs. Sylvia Bishop says that when she worked as a nurse in the geriatric wards in the hospital in the late1960s the patients were often badly treated by untrained nurses, some old people were charged for having a bath, their hair washed or for extra food, they didn't know that there wasn't a charge.

There was a maternity unit that was available to anybody and respectable women were well treated, but girls who were unmarried (and some were regular visitors) were treated very roughly. Some of the things that happened sickened the young nurses but it was difficult to complain. There was usually an influx of girls there nine months after the fair had visited the town. Some of them didn't fetch their babies until they were three months old! Some children even stayed until they were five, the nurses thought that they were safer there. There was still a Master and Mistress in charge and a Part-free system operated, it seems to have been a hangover from the workhouse system. People could stay for bed and breakfast for two shillings and sixpence a night and some work in the kitchens. If they had no money they worked until lunchtime. Sylvia went into one of the wards and saw that the men's shoes were each under a bed leg. She was told that they would otherwise have been stolen! It was usually the homeless and infirm who used the system. Some people were permanently housed in a block there, perhaps having been put in the Workhouse for some misdemeanour. One man who they called 'Toast' was put there when he was ten for an assault, he was still there 60 years later, he pushed the trolleys around. He didn't know what he was there for but was quite happy. Women could be detained there for having an illegitimate baby and stayed on if they had nowhere else to go. Some simple people were there for lack of somewhere to go.

In spite of having to try to keep a lot of rules, the nurses managed to have some fun, and got up to pranks. If they were late back at night they waited until the Porter had gone away then climbed over the big iron gates to reach the nurses home!

The Grand Turk and silk weaving
Scott Pettit's family are associated with the **Sutton Road** area near the Workhouse on more than one account. They were responsible for the building of The Grand Turk, and surrounding buildings and also for being prominent in the silk weaving industry. They would have been among the last to ply the trade.

Thomas and Eliza Paget   Courtesy of Scott Paget

This part of Sutton Common would appear to have been a silk weaving area, a relative, Joseph Martin is recorded there in an Indenture as early as 1810 as a 'Bombazeen Weaver', when he takes Mary Middleton, aged 15 years of Abberley as an apprentice. The 1841 census shows Scott's ancestors Joseph and Thomas Paget working as Silk Weavers. Thomas Paget, opened the Grand Turk in Sutton Road as a Public House in 1854, he was described as a Publican and Silk Weaver in the Census of 1861. He also built a row of cottages behind the Pub that became known as Grand Turk Row and probably also built the Grand Turk Villas. The cottages were demolished to make way for the bungalows on the right-hand side of Washington Street (when approached from Sutton Road). The path that led up to the cottages may still be seen, separating the Grand Turk Public House and the Grand Turk Villas.

The Grand Turk cottages housed silk weavers too, and it is particularly interesting to find that his relatives were plying the trade so late in the period when it was thought that silk weaving was finished, the latest record being in 1891. Another silk weaver, Benjamin Bradley is recorded living at Back of 28 Washington Row at the same time.

Another character in the **Sutton Road** that Scott has brought to my notice is that of **George Bradley** 1865-1938. A brief history of his life, gleaned from his obituary, describes a different kind of life and business in the town, one lived close to horses and wagons 'Gee-up' and horse manure! There were then local coal pits, deliveries to the house, with the thud of the bag of coal being tipped into the 'coal place', and coal smoke emitting from most house and factory chimneys. The canal wharves were busy with the unloading of coals and other supplies from the barges.

George Bradley was born in Trinity Lane in 1865 but his family were living in Sutton Road by 1881. In 1896 he is recorded in Kelly's Directory as a haulier, living at 70 Sutton Road. He moved to his final address at 175, Sutton Road in 1916 where the wide drive adjacent to it can still be seen, it led to the yard where he kept his wagons and later his lorries. George had worked for several carpet manufacturers before taking over his father's haulage business.

Among the many enterprises he served with his horses and wagons, and later his lorries, was hauling coal from the pits at Rock and Old Rockmoor (the Old Hall pit at the bottom of Clows Top Bank), and the Elan Valley Water Scheme for the City of Birmingham, when they were laying pipes on the long stretch from Cleobury Mortimer to Iverley, near Stourbridge. He had 45 horses at that time. He was engaged to transport materials for the new wing at the Infirmary and also the enlargement of St. John's Church. He had two boats on the canal ferrying coal from Cannock. Farming was one of his interests, he owned Whytlench Farm at one time and no doubt grazed his horses there.

The Larches

Thomas Hallen built the house known as 'The Larches' he was living there in 1827 and was a solicitor and Town Clerk of Kidderminster.

George Butcher a carpet manufacturer, moved to The Larches in 1834. He was the nephew of Thomas Lea the spinner, of Blakebrook Cottage. He adopted the name of Lea when he married into the family. The Lodge to the house still stands on the corner of Larches Road, the drive to the house was on the other side of the cottage, and Larches Road roughly parallels it. The house stood high above and had gardens, tennis courts and a bowling green behind. Summer fetes were held in the gardens. On the opposite side of Larches Road was the Coach house and stables facing behind a lane to take the coach to the stables. A bungalow near the traffic lights was home to the gardener. By Foley Park School was the dower house to the Larches. Mrs. Greatwich used to live in the Dower House, she usually wore black clothes and long earrings. She was a kindly lady who became something of a recluse.

The **Larches Auxiliary Hospital** was opened in Larches House on May 29th 1915. It contained 100 beds and was in use until April 30th 1919.

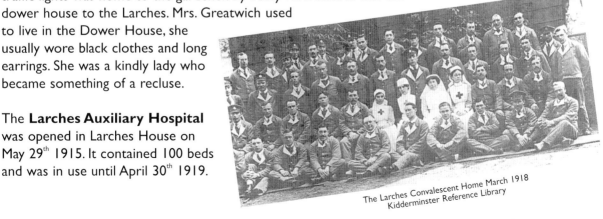

The Larches Convalescent Home March 1918
Kidderminster Reference Library

Members of the Red Cross detachments who came from Kidderminster, Bewdley and Wolverley staffed the hospital. The photograph shows convalescent soldiers being cared there in 1919.

Afterwards it became a private club for playing snooker, tennis and bowls. Though only half of the house was used.

The Larches wasn't the only large house built or inhabited by manufacturers in the carpet trade in the Sutton Common area as **Nigel Gilbert** details in his book *Ridiculous Refinement*. Most have been demolished by now, but the following have at sometime had carpet trade connections; Greatfield Hall occupied the Great Field, The Cedars opposite the Police Station was originally Blakebrook Cottage and is now Kemp Hospice, Woodfield House in Bewdley Street, Beechfield in Habberley Road, Summerhill 1 & 2 on Bewdley Hill; (part of No. 2 is in the Gainsborough Hotel. The No. 1 site is occupied by the petrol station.)

Church Mission

With the population increasing, the Church of England and the Primitive Methodists raised money in the 1880's in order to provide services for members and seekers who lived at the Foley Park end of the common. The Methodist chapel was the first to be built in 1885, followed three years later by Sutton Park Mission Church.

Foley Park Methodist Church
(The Tin Church)

The little 'tin church' was built on the corner of Sutton Park Road as a Primitive Methodist Church. It was opened on Thursday the 12th of November 1885, when the preacher was the Rev. Richard Baxter. It closed in 1963 when the present Methodist church in Sutton Park Road was built.

The Little Tin Church

Nell Bond now 93, who still plays the organ for morning service, is the widow of Ron, a well-loved Local Preacher. She remembers the church fondly as having a very friendly group of members. The main room for the congregation was furnished with a platform, pews, an old organ and a piano. A solid fuel stove placed in the middle of the church provided heating, other heating was added later. Nell remembers the lively Sunday School Anniversaries with the children crowded on the stage singing their special hymns for the occasion.

The back room for meetings also had a piano where the choir practised. A 'get together' was held there every Monday evening. There was no kitchen until the 1960s and the toilet was outside.

The tree that was decorated for Christmas still stands on the green at the Stourport Road and Sutton Park Road junction. The chapel can be seen behind the tram, the services from 1898 until the demise of the tram service in 1929 would have been punctuated by the rattle of trams, for they were busy on Sundays taking people to Stourport. I am told that the chapel was at one time painted yellow.

The alteration to the junction of Sutton Park Road and Stourport Road in 1963 necessitated the demolition of the church. The present Foley Park Methodist Church where Nell is organist, was built at that time.

Sutton Road Mission Church

A wooden church known as Sutton Road Mission Church, stood on the piece of land in front of where **Holy Innocent's Church** stands today. The Mission Church was opened for worship on May 3rd 1888, services had been held in a house in Sutton Road previously. It was built very near to the Methodist 'Tin Church' and was succeeded by the more permanent building of 'Holy Innocent's Church.

Holy Innocent's Church

The church was built in 1937/8 as a daughter to St. John's Church, the builders were the Lacy brothers. People were asked to contribute 1/- for a brick.

William Whitcomb records the day of its consecration: "July 2nd 1938. The Church of Holy Innocents, near Brinton Park, was consecrated today by the Bishop. This church was made possible by the late Mr. John Humphreys who left a sum which has reached £2,000. The church is made to seat 300 people but the nave has been left so that it can be extended in the future to complete the design of the architect. The Rev. Bertie Roberts launched the public appeal for the new church with a gift of £500 and also gave the rood hanging from the Chancel arch."

Its style of worship has been regarded as 'High Church.' With its hall, lately rebuilt, it has provided a place of worship and fellowship, and provided accommodation in the hall for all kinds of youth activities, playgroups, rummage sales, bazaars, meetings, talks and even temporary schooling in the last war! *(See page 33)*

The Tramway

Following the railway the trams came in **1898**. They ran from Comberton to Stourport. When the tram lines were first laid Melvyn Thompson says that there was just a sandy track to Stourport, when the winds blew the track could become covered, stopping the trams and even causing derailment. A ride on a tram was initially very popular for a day out, being crowded at holiday times. People would avail themselves of the steamboats on the River Severn. The open-sided trams were called **Toast Racks**. The trams gradually became less popular with the coming of buses, the track was closed in 1927.

HUME STREET BOARD SCHOOL

The school was founded in 1877 and closed in 1980s when it was used as a store for Educational furniture and later for the County Museum. It was an Infant School with only two classrooms. I'm told that the building was a poor one and people's memories of the lavatory accommodation of the two planks and a hole in the ground, was that they were horrible! The boys' urinal had slate panels and only one toilet. The headmistress was a teaching head with one assistant. The infants from St. Johns School in Chapel Street/Bewdley Road were transferred there in 1925 when their building was condemned as unsuitable. David and

Miss Hampton with her class 1920s   Courtesy of Gil Edwards

Beryl Gaston remember their time there in the 1930s when the head mistress was Miss Stewart, she was assisted by Miss Long and Miss Hampton. There was a good atmosphere in the little school, the teachers treated the children kindly. Although the school was for 'mixed infants', the boys and the girls had separate playgrounds. Beryl remembers going to Brinton Park for the annual Empire Day celebration on May 24th 1940, when the school sang patriotic songs and saluted the flag, the flag being attached to one of the goal posts!

Courtesy of Beryl Gaston

The photograph shows Hume Street infants, together with older pupils from St. John's schools when they gave a concert at the Town Hall in 1937 or 8. Beryl is in the middle.

FOLEY PARK SCHOOL

The School was built in 1894 to accommodate the growing number of children in the area it was extended in 1938. Unfortunately theLog Books were not available. The authorities could not have envisaged how necessary the extra space would become in 1939 when the evacuees arrived!

An evacuee
Ken Brooks tells how at ten and a half, he was one of fifty children with teachers, Mr. Jones (with his wife) and Miss Sheward, evacuated from Smethwick in Birmingham at the beginning of World War II. Ken was billeted on Mrs. Pavey in Larches Road for a short time. As she had a baby due he moved to another house in Neville Avenue to Mr. and Mrs. Cedric Humphries, who were good to him, Mr. Humphries was a carpet weaver. The houses were reached through a lane at the side of Park Inn. He settled in well, liking the country atmosphere in contrast to Smethwick. Though the children didn't stray far from Foley Park for fear of getting lost! They wore two red tags to identify them as being evacuees.

The children spent the first six weeks doing lessons in Holy Innocents' Church hall, before they were transferred to Foley Park School, however he was not there long before he moved to Coventry Street School for three months and then to the newly opened Kidderminster Modern school, later known as Harry Cheshire School. The school had received a hit from a bomb, the

Birmingham Evacuees 1939   Courtesy of Ken Brooks

resulting shortage of classrooms meant that the children, evacuees and resident, were catered for by the expedient of having them attending mornings or afternoons. The boys alternated with the girls, attending 8-12 one week and afternoons the next. Materials were in short supply and much of the time seems to have been spent in doing practical work such as putting in concrete footings in for a house for their teacher Mr. Joe Foxall! Ken says that it was fortunate that he had already learned to read and write. (Another ex-pupil remembers being asked to carry planks to the same teachers' house in St. Johns Avenue and to drop them in the garden, yet another said that classroom windows were often broken when he hurled tools toward misbehaving pupils! This would be when the woodwork room was at Radford Avenue.)

Ken joined the Reservoir Scouts KD 14. The Scout Master was Roger Sly. They built a Headquarters at the Reservoir. He remembers that they completely emptied the Reservoir, painted the bottom white and then filled it up again to enable the A.R.P. (Air Raid Precautions) to use the water supply. He remembers too that there were two old trams in Lisle Avenue that were later cut up for the iron to be melted for the war effort.

In 1942 his parents were bombed out of Smethwick, they came to live in Franche so the family stayed in Kidderminster permanently. He went to work then and had a series of temporary jobs at the various carpet factories when they were producing munitions for the war effort.

ST. JOHN'S SCHOOLS

St. John's First and Middle schools opened as a new Junior School in September 2007. The school buildings are sited in Blakebrook, but originally they were built nearer to the church.

St. John's School built 1850   Courtesy of Roy Bagnall

The school building in the grounds of St. John's Church in Brook Street is the one that was built for girls in 1884. The original school was the Chapel Street building that fronted Bewdley Street (now Road), and according to the Rev. J. R. Burton it was built in 1835, this preceded the church that was built during1837/38. He stated that the Chapel that gave its name to Chapel Street was built by Methodists, and according to Ebenezer Guest 'had come into the hands of John Woodward with some land in 1834, when the Roman Catholic's vacated it. He endowed it to be used as a 'nursery' by the people of St. John's Church. The 1859 map of Kidderminster shows the boys and girls school as an L shaped building on the corner of Chapel Street and Bewdley Street. It appears to have housed girls in one part of the building, with the boys in another part while the infants were in the Chapel. This was before the St. John's Infant's School was built in 1850 in St. Johns Street. Sometime before 1868 the girls had joined the infants there, the latter were transferred to the Chapel Street School during that year. The boys moved to St. Johns Street when the girls moved to their new school in Brook Street in 1884. When a fire occurred in the Girl's School in 1865 and they were reported as going to the 'old girl's school' it was probably to the Chapel Street site where the boys were at that time. The Infants moved to the Hume Street School building in 1925 when the Chapel Street school building was condemned.

ST. JOHN'S GIRLS' SCHOOL 1862

The first Log Book written in 1862 is a neatly hand written diary covering fifteen years, with a comment for each day, the Inspectors Reports are not so easily read! The first page encourages the reader to read on, for the third entry of the mistress **Miss M. Starr** on November 5th states:

> "Large numbers of children ask to leave early because parents had pigs killed on this day".

Slaughter House Peel Street   Kidderminster Reference Library

Many people living in the area kept pigs in their back yard and would have employed the 'pig killer' to come and do the necessary killing. There would have been much squealing, smell and mess, and obviously the children didn't want to miss the excitement! The photograph shows the abattoir in **Peel Street**, which was probably where the deed was done.

Staffing

Reading on we learn that the staff consisted of the Mistress, **Miss Starr**, two Pupil teachers **Emily Mann** and **E. Jackson**, **E. Tyrer** and **E. Baldwin** were two Monitors, one unpaid. If one of them were ill a girl from the top class, whom would be at the most twelve years old, would take the class. (Elizabeth Tyrer is shown as living in St. Johns Street in the 1861 census.)

At this time the Master or Mistress would usually have come to the school fresh from the Teacher Training School and be in their early twenties. The Pupil Teachers and Monitors assisted them. Pupil Teachers usually started at about fourteen years of age and Monitors two years earlier. The former served a

Extract from St. John's Girl's School Log Book

form of apprenticeship leading to a placement in Training School if they proved suitable. Miss Starr, on top of teaching a class and supervising the rest of the school, had to prepare the Pupil Teachers for their examinations for entry into a Teacher's Training School and also for their class teaching, she would do this for an hour before or after school. Miss Starr was just out of Training College, it being her probationary year. The Inspector in his report at the end of the year wrote that she had made a good start.

There was some outside help and support however, the Vicar or one his Curates intended to open school with prayers and gave some scripture and catechism lessons too, but quite often they were unable to attend. The Misses Annie and Isabella Lea, daughters of the carpet manufacturer, Mr. Henry Lea, who lived at Whitville Cottage, Franche, and at this early period a Miss [Mary] Winnall from Blakebrook, came to inspect the sewing or writing, to hear reading and perhaps read to the girls while they were sewing in the afternoons.

In January **1863**, the first day of occupying the Infant School (this appears from a subsequent entry, to have been in the two small classrooms in St. Johns Street), 40 new scholars were admitted.

Mary Westwood was mentioned as being a paid Monitor in November of that year. She was the daughter of Henry and Maria who kept the Woodfield Tavern, (mentioned above) and was aged but 10 years. It is of interest to note that she went on to become the Mistress of **St. Mary's Infant's School** and was so for 44 years, noted for her kindness to the children. In 1881 she was lodging with Miss Catherine Bailey, the Mistress of **St. Mary's Girls School**, by 1891 she lived at No. 10 **Summer Place** and in 1901 in **Habberley Street** with her sister and invalid brother.

Marching to keep warm

The Girl's School buildings had a large and a small room. The large room, with a gallery housed all the classes, while the 'classroom' was used for the infants or sometimes as a withdrawing room to teach a class or group on its own. Miss Starr writes of having five classes in the Large Room. A stove heated it, but the winters of the 1860's appear to have been very cold with snow and ice. Miss Starr wrote that the stove gave out so little heat that she was obliged to march the girls around between lessons because it was so cold. It also seemed to be particularly wet, for the attendance was often very low for that reason. In the early 1860s there were about 130 on roll but often only 70-90 arrived in time for prayers at 9 a.m., some arriving later.

At that time many children were short of clothing and poorly shod, the roads had poor surfacing and were covered in mire, (a report stated that the householders spread the ash from their fires and other rubbish on the roads and where else they could, this added to the horse dung) so while it was sometimes accepted that they could not attend, the teacher quite often sent for the absentees.

Schooling wasn't free

Attendance was still theoretically voluntary before **1870** and couldn't be strictly enforced until **1880** when sufficient places had been found for all children. However schooling wasn't free. The girls had to bring their pence to school and were sent home for it if they didn't bring it, sometimes they didn't come back. It was likely that there was no money in the house. In the 1860s there was great poverty in the town, many people had moved elsewhere for work. The charge appears to have been 2 pence a week at this time but went up over the years by a penny at a time. Free schooling wasn't general until 1918.

Standards

The children were arranged in Standards, Standard I being the top class. However 'classes' were numbered in reverse. Class I being the younger children. They were placed in their classes by attainment and size, so it was possible to be promoted early through the school to the top. Later this method was criticized, as some children didn't have the stimulation received in the higher forms never being able to reach the top.

Curriculum

So what did the girls learn? They were supposed to be at school in time for prayers at 9 a.m. In this period when they were late, the extra time was added on at the end of the morning. They had arithmetic, writing, spelling, reading, scripture, catechism, dictation, transcription, geography, singing, and occasional history lessons, the latter two in the afternoons, but sewing and drawing were more usual then. The girls went to the boy's school for drawing where they sometimes misbehaved! There was an annual art examination, some of them taken at the Corn Exchange or the new **School of Art**, in order to gain a place in the latter. Art was being particularly encouraged because of the importance for the carpet trade of technical drawing and design.

Work was usually done on slates but the older children were sometimes given paper to copy their work onto. The first time a class worked their sums on paper was carefully noted. It is noticeable that the Mistress used the Log Book very reverently, never making a mistake or wasting a line of a page. Slates were taken home to be washed and to do 'home lessons' on. I know that it was quite common to use 'spit rags' to clean the slates in school, the rags being collected up and put together in a tin afterwards, a useful breeding ground for the infectious illnesses that were rampant at the time! The top classes were pleased when copybooks arrived for them. These were used to practise their penmanship.

The Misses Lea of Franche assist with the sewing work

Sewing was important to the girls, they did not have access to many ready-made garments and most would be cut from hand me downs. The mothers could join a club that allowed them to purchase the garments at the end of the year when the girls usually had to forgo their other lessons in order to finish them. Often there was a shortage of sewing work to do, the school relied upon good ladies like the Misses Lea of Franche and others who came in with sewing work cut out ready to sew. (St. Mary's School depended on the Misses Lea too!) Some of the parents complained if the children did other lessons in the afternoon.

Chinese Curiosities

There were however occasional diversions, in June 1863 Miss Starr writes "Many boys and girls paid a halfpenny each to come in school at 4 o'clock to see some Chinese Curiosities exhibited by a Captain who had brought the things back from China himself." I expect that the event would have seemed very special to the children at that time.

Pupil Teacher honoured

At a period when teachers are viewed as being perhaps necessarily stern, an entry suggests a good relationship with a pupil teacher. "Allowed the whole school to go out to play for a quarter of an hour in the afternoon because the I & II class girls wished to give E. Tyrer her birthday presant [sic] from them viz A wreath of flowers which she wore while they were at play."

Saints' holidays

On St. John's Baptism Day the girls went to a service at St. John's Church, and had the rest of the day as holiday. Ascension Day was celebrated at St. Mary's Church, the 'mother church'. The girls were expected to assemble for Sunday School on Sundays.

Annual Treat and half-holidays

There was an Annual Treat on a Saturday, in May when the girls usually visited Habberley Valley and had tea. They sometimes went there also on a sunny afternoon. The attendance was always poor when the circus or the fair came to town or the horse races were run. Sometimes a half-holiday was given for the circus and fair. Surprisingly to us today, elections were a cause for excitement and absence. In September 1863 it is noted "A grand wedding took place at St. Mary's Church at 9 a.m. many parents took their children to see it". Only half the usual number of girls arrived in time for prayers at nine. The excitement was caused by the marriage of Emily and Cecilia the daughters of William Butler Best of Blakebrook House: a Magistrate and Yarn Agent, to the brothers William and Henry Oldham.

Discipline

It is not clear when the Mistress said that she had punished girls severely, what form that took, but mostly it would seem that the classes or individuals were kept for extra time to do their work again. Miss Starr reproved Miss M. Baldwin for "striking the little children in the classroom." Girls were occasionally sent home until they apologized usually for being stubborn or obstinate!

The Clothing Club

Sewing was a very important activity in the girl's school when most clothes were either 'hand-me-downs' or hand sewn. The entry in December **1864** gives detail about the clothing club: "No school in the afternoon because their parents assembled at 3 p.m. to receive the worth of the money they had paid in the clothing club, which was either the clothes made by the girls in school or an order to purchase things from the shop they preferred."

A New Mistress

In January 1865 Miss **Catherine Tustin**, Certificated Teacher from Gloucester and Bristol Training College [Fishponds] took charge of the school after the resignation of Miss Starr. She was apparently also straight from college. She was soon reporting "a very deep snow", she allowed some of the children to stay in school for dinner but ink was spilled on some of her books and the culprit could not be found, so she forbade any staying for dinner again.

Inspector's Report

After a lot of effort on Miss Tustin's part, the Inspectors report in May stated:

> "The order is fair. The failures were numerous among many of the children examined in the lowest Standard. My Lords have awarded a Grant to the Girl's School without reduction with considerable hesitation. Next year they will expect a great improvement in the Arithmetic of the Female Scholars."

Evening Classes

By October it is apparent that the Mistress also had a Night School to contend with. This appears to have been staffed by the Mistress and volunteer teachers. The boys met separately. Not surprisingly she sometimes found herself the only teacher present with as many as 47 girls. On other occasions the attendance was very poor. She complained of the street boys throwing stones. The girls had Arithmetic, sewing and drawing and sometimes sang hymns, the work resulted in most of them being presented for an examination. The girls were probably working in the carpet factories in the daytime and could be as young as ten years of age. The fact that their attendance was erratic was partly on account of the weather, but also on account of the erratic working hours in the factories, where overtime was worked to 'finish the piece'.

In spite of the Mistress being overworked, her Pupil Teacher **Eliza Mann** gained a 1st Class Scholarship for Fishponds Training College in Gloucester.

School on fire!

On Sunday October the 29th **1865** the school was partly burned, it was reported that the children assembled in the old Girl's School in Chapel Street, and were able to return to the 'Infant's' School two weeks later.

Christmas Tree and presents

After the Christmas holiday, on the 10th of January **1866** there was no school in the afternoon "as the room was required to dress the Christmas Tree for the children who were to receive their presents at 7 p.m." The result next day was: "Very few girls present at 9 a.m. being tired with their games and play of the previous evening."

On February 7th Mistress writes:

> "Sent part of the 4th class into 5th and part to 3rd for the Monitress could not govern them."

She also records "Miss Lea <u>who built these rooms</u> examined classes in Scripture." Probably the Lea family were benefactors of the school, which was the one in St. John's Street, for later it is recorded that "Miss Lea laid the foundation stone."

Miss Tustin was ill on the day of the Night School examination and didn't return until after the Easter holidays, the clergy and Pupil Teacher being in charge during her absence.

The H.M.I. Rev. **H. Sandford** inspected the school in May. He reported:

> " The tone and order of this school is good. The Arithmetic has improved though it still needs attention especially in the 4th standard."

Female Evening. The girls' Night School was also examined 41 girls were eligible for the examination The work of the school is said to have been injurious to the health of the hardworking mistress (Miss Tustin) but the results of the examination clearly show that the girls greatly need instruction." He concludes; "the number of children under 6 years old should be limited to 40 unless their instruction is separately provided for by the appointment of a female teacher."

Awnings, tickets and picnics

In June the girls sewed an awning for the yard, needed for the Sunday School, presumably in order to afford some shelter. In July they were busy making tickets for the Treat. There was poor attendance on the 10th because of The Weavers Picnic. In August some were away for the Foresters Picnic *(the Friendly Society?)* at Blakebrook.

Another New Mistress

In December **Caroline Tustin** resigned and Miss **Mary Ann Freeth**, again a Certificated Mistress from the Gloucester and Bristol Training College, took charge of the School in January **1867**. She was soon greeted by snowy conditions that lasted well into the month.

In the **1867** Report the Inspector wrote that the "girls are clean looking and intelligent children they are under better control than they were." After mentioning some Arithmetic failure he concluded: "There should if possible be an adult assistant as the number of young children is considerable."

In December evergreens were brought in to decorate the school for Christmas.

A Mistress for the Infant School in the Chapel Street buildings

In January **1868** Miss Matthews was appointed Mistress of the Infants. This would have relieved Miss Freeth of some responsibility However she was still responsible for girls of 7 years to leaving age, training the Pupil Teachers and Monitors and for the Night School. In March she reports: "The Infants leave the two class rooms to-day and will be taken to the School in Chapel Street." Now the infants and their Mistress were in a separate school, Miss Freeth, (who was about to receive her Certificate after her probationary period) staffed the girl's school with two Pupil Teachers. Mary Westwood as senior P.T. (now aged 15) would take over from the Mistress if she were away. There were at least 96 children on roll. On May 1st the Mistress "made a wreath of beautiful flowers for the children who were chosen to be Queens of the May". In the afternoon they went to **Habberley Valley.**

Habberley Valley - the place of school visits
Courtesy of Mr. & Mrs E Curry

The **Inspectors' Report** in July stated:

> "The Girls' School has improved since my last visit. The Mistress, Miss Freeth, shows kindness and animation in her manner as a teacher, and has her scholars in good order."

Apple Event

In September, Mistress and the Rev. C. N. Gray took 1st and 2nd classes to Habberley Valley, and to an orchard where Mr. Gray bought the girls apples. (Was there one for the teacher I wonder?) He was later in good books when he "hung beautiful pictures in the Large Room."

Noisy Mother's Meetings

In November Miss Freeth mentioned that, "Monday afternoon is not so quiet owing to the Mother's Meeting being held in one of the Classrooms." This was a room vacated by the Infants. It became a long-standing difficulty, making it difficult to maintain discipline with the cries of young children disturbing the lessons. She complained to the Managers but later found that both classrooms had been taken over by the Mother's Meeting.

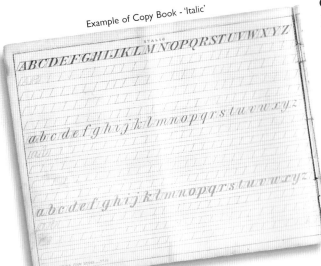

Example of Copy Book - 'Italic'

Clerical oarsman

In June **1869** the Rev. Gray surpassed himself, "he kindly took the 1st and 2nd classes to Eyemore Wood and to their great delight gave them a row for some miles down the Severn."

In September the Large Room curtain had to be lengthened to stop winter winds entering so freely. It is interesting to note that at that time there were swings in the playground, but in October they were locked up "because of disobedience with respect to them".

In April **1879** three of the girls in the 1st class were ambitiously working for a prize offered in the **Sunday Friend** for the best outline of Jewish History from the times of Moses to the death of Samuel!

Lack of teaching power

In the first months of **1871** Miss Freeth was beset with staffing difficulties. **Mary Westwood** gained a First Class Queen's Scholarship for entry to college, and **E. Gardner** had already gone to college. They were to have a new teacher in place of the latter. She notes that "**Emma Taylor** is a painstaking instructor" and promotes her to 2nd Class in the place of Mary. However "3rd Class is in great disorder **Emily Caswell** is not strong enough for a Pupil Teacher" but "**Emma Moore** is now Monitor of 4th Class and 'promises to become a good teacher."

In February she writes "It is difficult work, 118 children one Pupil Teacher and two 1st class Monitors. We are trying to get a new teacher, but it is not an easy matter. Then in March; "It is difficult to carry on the work of the school with so little teaching power. Several girls have tried schoolwork but we cannot get one to suit. The present 1st Standard is so large that the 3rd is moved into the 1st class so I must besides superintending whole school, teach the work of three Standards. It is almost impossible to do it as it should be done." Later the Pupil Teacher **Emma Taylor** had to take charge of the School because the Mistress was off sick. Miss **C. M. Bailey** from St. Mary's Girls School promised to help and took charge until Miss Freeth returned the following week. There were still staffing problems in August when the Mistress writes that she often had to leave 1st class in order to teach the 3rd Class.

In July some girls were sent home because they "would not pay the extra penny for the School Fee now 3d." Some parents complained consequently that they couldn't pay 3d. for a week when there was a days holiday in it. (Workers would not have been paid for the holiday.)

Tea with the Lea's!
One highlight of 1872 was when **Miss Annie Lea** invited eight girls to have tea on her lawn! She also promised to pay for a child's schooling.

1873 started with the usual bad weather, in February some girls were absent through bad chilblains, they couldn't get their shoes on. One afternoon in May, the girls were taken to **St. Mary's** new **Infant School** [in Horsefair] to an entertainment given by an **Arabian**, it was described as "very pleasant and informative."

By September the numbers on roll had increased and the teaching power was insufficient again. Miss Freeth resigned in December and a new Mistress, **Mary Haynes Burton** took charge in January 1874. Mary Burton was 21 years old and had come from the National School in Inkberrow.

(Attendance was low on March 23rd "in consequence of the Presentation of a Testimonial to **Mr. Henry Lea**, the father of Annie and Isobel.)

Mistress absent
Miss Burton reported on April. 2nd "I was obliged to leave the school in charge of Emma Taylor [a Pupil Teacher] being very unwell. I was absent from school for a fortnight, school - work was carried on by Emma Taylor and the Monitors assisted by Miss Jackson an ex Pupil Teacher. Resumed April 27th."

Not surprisingly the **Inspector reported:** "School not in efficient state Grant may be reduced."

Stabbed by a crochet hook
On September 9th Miss Burton reported:
"Lessons were disturbed this a.m. by an accident which happened to a girl. A crochet hook ran into her leg. She became faint and alarmed the children. A woman was sent for who extracted it."

At the end of December **Miss Burton** resigned after just one year. **Emily Mann** an ex Pupil Teacher became the new Mistress in January 1875. She was away through illness the first week, but reported the school in order. The Vicar endorsed her opinion later in the month. (Emily had not been to Training College.)
In March some girls who were 'half-timers' (those who were old enough to work for a half day, but must by law attend school for the other half) left St. John's School because it was their employers choice that they should go the **New Meeting School**. Carpet manufacturers were often non-conformists.

Attendance was not good one day in April owing to the excitement of some soldiers coming into town. On July 26th there was a half days holiday for the unveiling of the **Richard Baxter** statue.

The girls are photographed
In October there is the first mention of the children having their photograph taken. It is a pity that the original photograph has not been found.

Measles, eye infections and Scarlet Fever

1876/77 saw widespread attendance problems through recurrent Measles epidemics, eye problems and Scarlet Fever. In November 1877 the Mistress was still reporting "breakings out of Bad eyes and Measles". There were problems with the heating, the man from **Welsh's** in the High Street had to come to lengthen the pipe of the stove to make the fire burn. Also the roads to the school were "very bad indeed which lead to the school in consequence the girls get their feet wet."

Miss Mann suffers 'overwork'

On January 21ˢᵗ **1878** Miss Mann reports that she was: "Absent most of the week in bed attended by **Dr. Jotham**. He said that she was suffering from 'overwork' and did not allow her to return until February though she did the registers and cut out needlework and the teachers reported every day." She went back when her head Pupil Teacher **Madeline Darricot** had Influenza and reports; "Great many away with bad throats, two children died."

Prizes for needlework

Miss Lea visited in March to look at the needlework and promised four prizes for the best work.

In his June Report the Inspector wrote:

> "The girls are orderly as regards instruction, amount and quantity obtained are better than style and quality repetition for instance, was very thoroughly   known, but the meaning of the words very rarely understood. More desks are needed."

Cane not permitted

Miss Mann made several complaints about the cane being used in school.
In September the **Rev. H. B. Vale** was presented with a silver pencil case as a small mark of gratitude and affection for him.

Mistress marries

In October the teachers and children presented Miss Mann with a Copper Tea-Kettle on the occasion of her marriage. She finished her tenure at the school in December.

An honest girl

Also in October she reported "Agnes Cope returning from an errand to the Co-op picked up a bag with £20 in it in Gold and Silver, The honest child (and parents) returned it with pleasure to the small shopkeeper; who was in great distress, she was searching the streets with her friends; carrying lighted candles. Mrs. ----- who had lost the Cash, gave the child 2/6d. for a reward."

A new Mistress and an Assistant Mistress

1879 started with a new Mistress **Miss M. A. Probert**. The average number in attendance being 158, an Assistant Mistress, **P. Turner** joined her in mid-February, taking charge of Standard II. Also in February the girls were treated to a visit to the Town Music Hall to see a **"diorama of the War"** exhibition.

Miss Probert asks for water

In March the new mistress records: "I spoke [to the Managers] about water being laid on for drinking purposes." When this was supplied it was possible to do 'brushwork' as well as drawing.

There was still a great deal of illness affecting the attendance. The children are often away for long periods, being left very weak after the infectious diseases.

Some children left to attend the new Board School (Hume Street Board School) 'on Sutton Common'.

December saw the "presentation to the **Rev P. W. Brancker** with a mother-of-pearl paper knife and reader from the scholars and teachers."

Uncle shot

1880 began in January with a drama. The Mistress reports: "Gave permission for Louisa Pearsall to wait upon her Uncle who had been shot".
The Kidderminster Times of January 3rd reports that Thomas Pearsall, a Starcher, who lived at 63 Wood Street was in the **Sportsman Tavern** there on the 22nd of December when Alfred Partridge (who had served 10 years in the army) came in. Pearsall, who was in the taproom, offered him a drink from the jug, but Partridge took out his revolver and shot him in the chest, the landlady said "Oh! Mr. Pearsall", Mr Pearsall said: "I've been shot Missus". Partridge escaped from the tavern but was later apprehended by Inspector Ebury at the Bridge Inn, where Partridge fired shots at the Detective and Elizabeth Clarke but missed. Pearsall was said to be improving. The Court case at Worcester was reported two weeks later. No motive was found for Partridge's actions, he was drunk at the time. Later it transpired that there were some family tensions. (Louisa was described as the daughter of Thomas and Mary on the 1881 Census, Thomas had survived.)

February saw the first mention of a **Library** when Miss Lea came to speak to the children about the Library, part of the first Class being allowed to subscribe.
Outbreaks of Scarlet Fever and swollen throats continued right into May.
The Mistress was having a great deal of difficulty with the poor teaching of the Pupil Teachers, she often had to leave her own class to attend to their classes. In June the **School fees were raised to 4d**. Several children were removed to other schools. Five mothers came to say that they could not pay the extra. (The money was probably needed to pay for the assistant teacher.)

The **Inspectors Report** in July stated:

> "The discipline of the Girls' School is highly satisfactory the children being
> unusually quiet and attentive. They are still backward in their attainments,
> but there is evidence of progress and they now have a capable Mistress -."

Staffing problems

At the end of June the Assistant Mistress, P. Turner was replaced by Miss Owen an ex Pupil Teacher from St. Mary's School. She chose to return there in August, and was replaced in September by Miss S. Gale. The Mistress, Miss Probert soon found Miss Gale's class in a disorderly state, she resigned in October, being replaced by Julia Mann. After more difficulties and complaints from mothers (one mother accused Miss Mann of beating her daughter across the face with a cane), Miriam Probert resigned at the end of December, she was replaced by **Elizabeth Perry** Certificated Mistress in January **1881**. (Elizabeth Perry then aged 22 was a Boarder in Chapel Street in the home of Margaretta Morgan another National School Mistress.)

The year started with a "great lot of illness among the children" The **School Board**   and **Relieving Officers** put in an early appearance. The former being responsible for the children's attendance, and the latter gave money to families in real hardship and sometimes helped with school fees. The Vicar was still paying his usual visit in the morning. The entries for the first half of the year speak of the continuing illnesses, poor weather, disobedient girls and the struggle to have the knitting and sewing ready for examination time!

In June the Mistress writes: "The children pay their fees very irregularly now owing to the state of the trade in the town." That month the girls had a day off for the unveiling of the **Rowland Hill Statue**."

The **Inspector's Report** in July described the difficulties under which the school was working: "The school is in a critical state. The Arithmetic is worse than last year. The girls are very orderly and the reading and writing well done. One of the rooms should be fitted with desks. *[This suggests that the girls were sitting on forms.]* Part of the main room cannot be used because of an accumulation of chairs and other articles used in the Sunday School. There will be a reduction in the Grant."

As happens today sometimes, struggling schools had improvements made more difficult by money being withheld.

In the **Inspector's Report** he acknowledged the many difficulties that Miss Perry had encountered and though the school had not acquitted itself so successfully as in previous years felt sure her earnest care and perseverance would be rewarded next year. The Staff now comprised: Miss Elizabeth Perry C. M., Pamela Turner and Julia Mann Assistants, May Page Pupil Teacher 1st Year and Alice Alford Temporary Monitor. There were 220 pupils on roll. With Miss Turner being replaced by Miss Breakspear in August.

Dissolving views
In December "the children were taken to the Town Hall, to see some dissolving views. The treat was given by a gentleman of the town and was much enjoyed by the children."

By February **1882** measles and fever had broken out again in the neighbourhood, and the outbreak was still affecting the attendance in April.

In August Miss Perry wrote: "re-opened the school on Monday morning, [7th] so few children being present it being Bank Holiday that I closed the school." The school was left to the care of the other teachers for the next ten days there being "great trouble at home."

The **Inspector** wrote in April: **1883**
 "--- some progress has been made, but the results in many points hardly rise to mediocrity" after a detailed analysis of the various Standards' work, he conceded "The girls are now in good order."

In **1884** the school opened two weeks late because of "the **breaking out of smallpox** in the town." Subsequently there was an outbreak of 'bad' or 'dirty' heads making "girls unfit to sit with others".

On May 30th **Elizabeth Perry resigned**. On June the 9th **E. Gardner** took charge of the school, she was styled Head Mistress, a reflection of the fact that she had Julia Mann a Certificated Teacher under her.

In June there was a further outbreak of Measles in the neighbourhood. In September Miss Gardner wrote: **"[Typhoid] fever** broke out, many of the children are ill and many have relations suffering from it. Kate Laycock [the Stipendary Monitor] has it." She returned a month later.

In August the **H.M.I.** wrote of the April inspection:

> "--- the Girls are making creditable progress in the lower Standards but the elder scholars are still in an unsatisfactory condition".

 In October the Diocesan Inspector was able to place the school in 'First Class', though with some qualifications. The Diocesan Inspectors were always more generous in their reports. Miss Mann the assistant, left in December to take charge of a small school.

In January **1885** the children took part in an entertainment the proceeds were to go to the New School Building Fund.

Miss Jervis C. M. replaced Miss Mann as Assistant, and the fever made an unwelcome return, as it did again in March.

Brook Street School

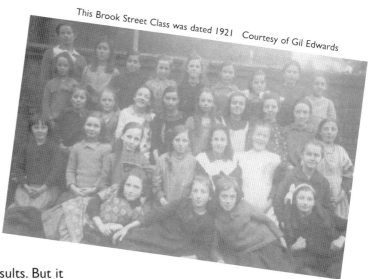

This Brook Street Class was dated 1921   Courtesy of Gil Edwards

On June 8th Miss Gardner wrote: "Recommenced work but in the new school in Brook Street." This is the building that still survives today.

The **H.M.I.'s Report** states: "The past year has been marked by a serious epidemic of typhoid fever, which has doubtless done the Girls' Department a considerable amount of injury. Allowance has been made for this drawback in estimating the merit of the instruction and the results. But it is only too obvious that the children are not trained to reason or observe, their work being absolutely mechanical and devoid of intelligence. Much of the writing is neat and regular. The Reading is fluent, but the Girls are seldom able to give the meanings of words in the passages read, Arithmetic is done in a mechanical fashion, Mental Arithmetic being almost unknown. …. Recitation, Discipline and Sewing deserve commendation."

This kind of comment was repeated many times throughout Miss Gardner's tenure. No doubt she, her Pupil Teachers and Monitors had also not been taught to think.
The Diocesan Report however was "Excellent. I wish all Church Schools had buildings like this."

In June the work of the school was hindered by a large stage owned by a drama company taking up a lot of space in the Large Room.

Children hurting
From June onwards there were various complaints by mothers of the Pupil Teacher Kate Laycock hurting their children. Her indentures were eventually cancelled by mutual consent. The complaints were then vented on Alice Alford who seriously bruised a girl, in spite of being forbidden to hit the children by Miss Gardner. She survived however to take her Scholarship examination.

Staff problems
In January 1887 Miss Ibell joined the staff as Assistant but could not manage Standard IV and left after two weeks. Miss Downes came in her stead but after many complaints of her beating girls in the two weeks that she was there, the Vicar terminated her engagement on the morrow. Miss Bowie was a more permanent replacement.

Golden Jubilee
On June 24th **Queen Victoria's Golden Jubilee** was celebrated. The girls assembled to enjoy the feast provided for them on the Monday. There was a whole holiday on Tuesday so 'only half fees were taken from them.' Brinton Park wasn't handed over to the town until August 1st although it was a 'Jubilee gift' from John Brinton, it was to be the venue for subsequent royal celebrations and much more.

The **Inspector** that year continued the complaint:
> "--- that the children's fingers and memories are well trained, but the Teachers unfortunately fail to lay sufficient stress on the development of the reasoning and observing powers."

Winter diseases start again
In November Scarlet Fever and skin disease were prevalent. The new Assistant, Miss Hill resigned after one month, being unable to take a large class. Miss Gardner divided Standard III into three parts with the Assistants and Mistress taking one part each. At the beginning of 1888 Scarletina broke out, Ada Lowe a Monitor was away for six weeks recovering from it.

The **H.M.I.s Report** that year was more encouraging as progress had been made in some areas, this he judged was commendable since the three Pupil Teachers were all in the 1st year of their training. The **Diocesan Report** had quite a lot of nice things to say, of the 1st Division he said: "I have but rarely examined a brighter or nicer class. The School is in excellent order and has about it a very nice tone."

In December 25 prizes given by **Michael Tomkinson** (the Carpet Manufacturer) were distributed.

In July 1889 some girls were in the hospital with Fever and one little girl died of consumption.

The Vicar was trying to make arrangements for the girls to attend a class for **Practical Cookery**. The girls had their first lessons in September. 48 went for a Demonstration in the morning and 24 for a Practical one in the afternoon.

The **H.M.I. reported**:
> " --- the girls are certainly inferior to their brothers in point of accuracy and intelligence. - Reasoning and observing faculties have hardly received due attention."

Diseases and closures

In November the epidemics of measles and fever had become very serious, the situation continued into January **1890** when the school had to be closed for a week because staff and children had influenza and colds. The school experienced "a considerable loss in fees in consequence of the epidemics." In March Miss Leigh an Assistant Teacher was taken ill, she returned to school after three days but was quite unfit for work as she had Hysteria. She resigned and was allowed to leave at once.

The **H.M.I.s Report** for 1890 cited:

> "Progress - remarkable and creditable - but still neatness with mechanical accuracy."

This was in spite poor attendance through epidemics and Pupil Teachers who didn't prepare their lessons.

Miss E. Read, a Pupil Teacher boxed a girl's ears although she knew she had gatherings in them. She further did badly in her quarterly papers. Subsequently Miss Gardner complained to the Vicar about her carelessness with the registers and other things. She was reprimanded for sending frivolous letters to another teacher, but in spite of her problems she later passed Second Class in the Scholarship examinations.

Chess Tournament

An interesting entry in July states that "A half holiday was given on Wednesday in order that eighteen of the girls might take part in the Chess Tournament at St. John's Social Gathering."

Workhouse children

In **1892** the year started with a severe snowstorm. The Mistress had influenza. Later in January she wrote: "The Managers have decided that the girls from the Workhouse are to attend our school. Seven were admitted. Their Arithmetic is very poor indeed." Three days later nine more girls were admitted. She found that: "as a rule they read quite well, write fairly and are very weak in Arithmetic." (They would have previously been taught at the workhouse.) The Mistress said that many of the girls who had returned from illness were in a weak state.

In February an epidemic of Measles had broken out in the workhouse, and the Vicar wished all the children from that institution to be sent home at once. This was soon followed by an outbreak of Fever. At that time other children in a family where there was measles had to stay at home.

The **H.M.I.s Report** was on his usual lines but he added

> "Standard I children should be taught to clean their slates with sponges."
> Soon after an "Organizing Visitor" gave a generous report of the work of the school and "was much pleased with the excellent order, and with the tone and hearty spirit of the school."

Teachers' Treat

There was a new enterprise in September when a days' holiday was given "in order that the teachers might join those of the other Department in an excursion to Witley."

1893 started with woe: "The ice in the pipes has now melted, and as a consequence part of the principal room and half of the classroom are flooded. It is extremely uncomfortable for the children."

On April 14th Miss Gardner reported that she had been absent all the week by permission of the Managers. There were no entries by Miss Gardner after the 17th of April, her last entry was "Our staff of teachers is very poor at the present. We are in want of two Assistants. She had served nine years as Mistress.

Lucy Alis Rogers
The next entry on June 12th is "Commenced work as mistress of this school, 219 girls present. [Signed] Lucy Alis Rogers."

As will be seen this turned out to be a momentous day for the school.

On the 14th of June she received a note from the Master of the Union to say that the Guardians of the Union had accepted an invitation for the children to attend the Agricultural Show. She boldly queried why they had to go in the morning when there was a half-holiday in the afternoon.

Making a firm groundwork
During her first week she thoroughly examined the school, then wrote a syllabus of guidance for the teachers. It instructed them upon how to teach as to produce more intelligent answers. She gave each teacher an examination book detailing the faults of each class, and gave advice as to the best methods of dealing with difficult subjects. The whole of the work was commenced with the idea of getting a firm groundwork for the coming year. She wrote in the Log: "The chief aim of nearly each teacher is to watch the clock. The teachers arrive at the last moment, and depart as early as possible." The teachers were now to be in the playground five minutes before 9 to see their classes into school.

The following week she wrote: "Have been compelled to speak very strongly to some of the teachers about carelessness and laziness. They complain of the disobedience of the children, but fail to use the means at their disposal for correction. They apparently have an idea that the only form of punishment is the cane."

Miss Rogers now had four Assistants only two were certificated. She used the younger teachers to assist the responsible teachers.

Tea at the Vicarage
On July 4th the top Standard were invited to tea by the Vicar, the Rev. J. F. Kershaw.
On the 6th there was a days holiday for the marriage of the **Duke of York and Princess May.**

On the 7th Mrs. Rogers writes: "Have spent a considerable portion of the time that I have been here in showing the teachers how to teach. They do not keep the children fully employed and sadly do not train the reasoning powers of the children." In September she reported: "The repulsive habit of **spitting on slates** is now nearly eradicated." By now Miss Clark and Miss Watson were 'most energetic' with their classes.
In October because of the depressed state of trade, many children were unable to bring their fees.

The **H.M.I. reported** in March **1894**: "The work of a capable and experienced Mistress has already had a beneficial effect on attainments, increased intelligence is shown."

A note in April shows that the salary at that time for a 12 years old Monitor was 1/6d. per week rising to 2/- at 13 years. (2 shillings was one tenth of a pound.)

School closed for disease

In the autumn the school was dogged by measles and fever again. In October the Sanitary Committee ordered the closure of the school.

In April **1895 Kate Bywater** was listed as a Candidate for training as a Pupil Teacher, she was accepted. She was to go on to teach in the Boy's department in 1899 when she finished her apprenticeship. She then gained a 2nd Class in the Queen's Scholarship Examination before entering Training College. Having finished her training she was to succeed **Miss Catherine Bailey** in 1904 as Head Teacher at St. Mary's Girl's School. (She was born in 1881. Her father William was a Market Gardener, her sister Amelia was also a pupil teacher, they lived in Hobro, Wolverley) **Eleanor Edwards** who started as a Pupil Teacher at same time as Kate, left the town but came back and succeeded **Mary Westwood** at **St. Mary's Infant's School** in 1917, bringing new ideas - 'freework' to the school.
In July Miss **Downes** who had joined the school as an'ex P.T.' was suffering from exhaustion after her week of examinations. She resigned in April **1897** after more illness and sadly died in late August.

Queen Victoria's Diamond Jubilee

Children were given two days holiday for the Jubilee on the 22nd and 23rd of July. "On the 22nd the children all had tea and were afterwards taken to **Brinton Park** where in conjunction with the other schools of the town they sang The National Anthem, The Old Hundredth and a specially composed song "Flash your Beacons" among others. The children were later presented with enamel mugs.

Training for Pupil Teachers

In September there was a new arrangement regarding the training of the pupil teachers. For some time they had been receiving instruction at Coventry Street Board School at various times in the week. Now they were to attend Central Classes at the School of Science. The Mistress wrote: "The deficiency of teaching staff upsets the organization to a very considerable extent." She was short of an Assistant at this time. The P.T.s were attending the Science School for Lectures only, the Mistress being responsible for their other lessons.

In October Miss Read was away with a 'gathered face' - and there were over 60 cases of measles. ['Gathered faces' were a common affliction for many years, the result of tooth abscesses.]

The **H.M.I.s report** of earlier in the year was glowing. He spoke of the highly efficient way in which Miss Rogers continued to instruct her school. The Diocesan Report was impressed by the intelligent way the girls had mastered the difficult subject of Reformation History, taught to them by the Rev. Spackman.

Continuing their extended education in January **1898** the older girls were taken to the Kidderminster Museum and in April some of the girls were taking part in an **Operetta** at the Town Hall.
On November 4th the school closed all day for the visit of **Barnum Bailey's Circus**.

Swimmimg

In June 25 girls went to the swimming baths in Mill Street having previously been given swimming drill at school by the Baths Instructor.

When school resumed in September after the summer holidays, Miss Rogers reporting on absences wrote: "11 are still at the seaside (no doubt cheap railway returns were responsible) and some are suffering from English Cholera."

In October the upper girls went to the Rev. Spackman's history lectures, they took place at the **School of Science** on Wednesday evenings.

Knitting for the Worcester's

In January **1900** the teachers and girls were reported to be knitting a quantity of caps and socks for the 2nd Worcester regiment, and the local Volunteers then fighting in South Africa.

Diphtheria

Three sisters were away because their little sister had died from diphtheria. The epidemic broke out also in the Union workhouse and the Infant School was closed because there were several cases there.

On March 1st there was a half-holiday celebrating the relief of **Ladysmith.**

The **Inspector reported** in June:

> " Elementary Science has been taught with much success. The behaviour of the Girls and their manifest interest in School Duties are not the least pleasing features of the Girl's School."

In September the girls were rewarded with a half-holiday to attend a **Wild Beast Show**.

Death of Queen Victoria

In **1901** it was reported that the operetta performance by the girls on January 22nd, at the Town Hall "when but half over was closed on account of the death of Her Majesty Queen Victoria." No doubt the schoolchildren were well aware of the Queens' funeral on February 2nd, when William Whitcombe wrote in his diary:

> "Wretched weather, snow all day for the funeral of Queen Victoria. there was a procession of mayor and Corporation to St. Mary's Church. All places of business with the exception of barbers and publicans were closed today many shops put up black shutters, flags were hung up draped and generally the whole town looked sober and wore an air of respect for the funeral of our beloved Queen."

In June the declaration of **'Peace in South Africa'** merited a half-holiday.

Coronation postponed

Holidays were altered again for Royal happenings. The usual Fair and St. John's Day holidays were not given because the holidays for the Coronation of His Majesty King Edward VII would last from the 25th to the 30th of June. It was announced on the 24th, that owing to the serious illness of the King the Coronation had been postponed. The children went to school as usual on the 25th and the 26th. Tea had been prepared by the Corporation to celebrate the coronation of the king: 'it was partaken of by the children in the afternoon, after which they were '*quietly* dismissed'.

(The Coronation eventually took place on August 9th. Mr. Whitcombe wrote: "Early service and then an hours ride to see the decoration round the town. went up to the Park ceremony. There was a very large crowd up there and we were just in time to see the bonfire lighted and the fireworks were let off on the hill adjacent to the Park the Town Hall was magnificent.")

Visit to the ruins of Harvington Hall

The Mistress took the majority of the girls in Standard 7 to the ruins of Harvington Hall in July. At that time the land opposite the school was acquired for outdoor drill purposes.

Playground paved

On August 25th it was noted: "During the holidays the interior of the Schoolroom has been coloured and varnished and the playground has been paved." The latter event was much needed the Inspectors had often remarked upon its necessity. October to December of that year was marked by many cases of both Measles and Scarlet Fever.

In **1903** Ada Whatley received a 1st Class for her examination result upon application to college, being 10th in a list of 2,000. She subsequently entered Tottenham Training College with a Grant of £5 in respect of her award.

A Lady of Literature

That year Lucy Rogers signed herself with L.L.A. after her name for the first time. The letters stand for Lady of Literature and Arts. While encouraging her girls to study hard she was obviously doing so herself.

New Authority

In April the school came under a New Authority, that being the Town Council of Kidderminster.

Wild West Show and - Tickenhill

In June summer activities are recorded: "Whole holiday for **Colonel Cody's "Wild West Show**", this was instead of a half holiday for the Fair." Later in the month Miss Campbell's class went to Bewdley: "to the historical building of **Tickenhill**", the Mistress took Standards 6 & 7 to the Kidderminster Museum.

Inventory of school furniture

An inventory had been taken of the school furniture in April, no doubt on account of the change of responsibility for the school. It comprised:

46 Large desks	6 Black boards, 4 Easels
3 Cupboards	1 Head Teacher's Desk
1 Table	1 Platform
4 Chairs	1 Clock
1 Notice Board	1 Waste Paper Basket

The large desks were long ones, Marjorie Sykes (nee Samuel) who remembers them, said that they seated six girls each. Note that only the Head Teacher had a desk, the other staff members obviously didn't even warrant a table!

The new Education Authority evidently deemed the provision insufficient, for in April of the next year Miss Rogers was very pleased to receive 'a large new cupboard'.

A Science Lecture

On November 20th the Mistress left early in order to take her turn in the cycle of teachers responsible for the order and behaviour of the Friday afternoon Science Class at the School of Art and Science. Mr. H. E. Hadley gave his lecture on "**Matter, Molecules, Density and Porosity**".

Excellent results

1904 started with excellent results from the Diocesan Scripture Examinations, when Pupil Teachers and Candidate: Nellie Wellings (was then 19 and living with her family at two Mill

Street), Nellie Parker and Dorothy Chambers gained three '1sts'. They were placed head of their respective years of apprenticeship.

The girls entered for outside examinations were regularly obtaining high marks in all areas. Miss Rogers was an able teacher in many subjects and passed on her knowledge to her pupil teachers and monitors, including Music, the girls became known for their singing. The Rev. Spackman, Vicar of St. John's Church also played a good part in the school by teaching not only Scripture in a way that interested the girls, but also in branching out into Reformation Studies and gaining their interest there. The Diocesan report for **1905** is copied below:

General Report

> *"I leave this school what I have always found it, a school second to none for the thoroughness of the work and the spirit in which it is done. Oral and written work alike, were of a high order of merit; the girls are intelligent and interested in their work, and the school is bound to be a great power in the district in which it is situated. It stands among the best schools in the Worcester Diocese."*
> [signed] John C. Whall
> Diocesan Inspector

In May in keeping with the usual spirit of enterprise 72 girls were taken to a **Trade and Art Exhibition** at Stourbridge.

In January **1906,** Mrs. Lomax was sent to the school by the Local Authority as a 'Supply Teacher', schools had hitherto relied upon borrowing staff from other schools when they were desperate.

In February the Mistress wrote that **Nellie Parker** had gained the 'Houghton Exhibition' (worth £7) for gaining the highest number of marks of any Pupil Teacher for 3 years, in the Diocesan examination, she went to Fishponds Training College in Gloucester in September. The school had the highest place for Pupil Teachers in each of the divisions.

Military Drill

In November **Captain Crawshaw** was appointed to instruct the teachers in the borough in Drill instruction, in order to secure uniformity of drill exercises among the teachers of the town. At that time drill was the usual form of exercise for both boys and girls, games were to be introduced later.

In December the staff received a half-holiday to assist in a large Rummage sale for the benefit of the **Poor Children's Boot Fund**. (The Fund had been started in 1901 by Supt. Bennett, it provided thousands of pairs of boots for poor children.)

Staffing problems

At the beginning of **1907** Mrs. Rogers was facing a staff crisis. She trained her teachers so well, (holding criticism lessons after school once a week for younger teachers to be advised by the rest of the staff,) that they often gained promotion to other schools. Some left to return to their hometowns for a better salary and others got married. Pupil Teachers left to go to Training College or sometimes moved away with their families. Added to that, they were now going to attend the training at the Science and Art centre full time for three terms during their apprenticeship.

The February Report by the 'Correspondent' **Rev. H. M. Spackman**, when her staff comprised 5 teachers and 4 Pupil Teachers, is sympathetic to her situation:

> "The girls' school is taught with great diligence, good methods and considerable success, but the following points require special notice. There is only one certificated assistant on the staff, and several of the teachers, though willing and capable, are inexperienced. The head mistress is consequently overburdened in endeavouring to attain to high proficiency throughout, as she has to exercise an unusual amount of supervision generally, while taking almost the whole work of the highest class herself. The discipline of the girls' department is admirable. Needlework, singing and arithmetic deserve unqualified praise."

The resignations continued during the year and new teachers were appointed. By December one of the teachers was suffering from "Mental and Physical overstrain" She later resigned having "secured a position with a higher salary."

Pay levels

An entry in the Log Book in October shows the differing rates of pay for teachers in adjoining counties. Miss Cox, an uncertificated assistant teacher whose present salary was £30 (per annum) was to receive £50 in Stourbridge. This difference obviously made recruitment difficult. Teachers were able to travel to nearby towns by train.

In July 1908 there was again an "excellent" Diocesan report. The best Scripture papers were by **Mary Wase Rogers** (the Mistress's daughter), **Maud Gaston**, and **May Griffiths**.

In December five girls are recorded as receiving 'breakfast tickets' and thirteen had boots from the boot fund.

The **Report by the H. M. I**. in April **1909** was as follows:

> "Girls premises. The cloakroom accommodation is inadequate. I understand the Managers will submit proposals for supplying the deficiency, and also for partitioning the main room. The lighting of Standard II classroom is not very good. More inlets for fresh air are needed. The long desks should never be more than five rows deep with proper gangways between each group. In many of the desks the seats are too far from the desks. There are only 5 closets for 252 girls."

French and Mathematics

Mrs. Rogers was always ready to add a subject to the curriculum if she saw a need. When French was added Gladys Whittingslow gained a distinction in French and Mathematics in the Preliminary Examination for entry to Tottenham Training College.

In **1910** the new **Inspector** in his **Report** noted:

> "There is a pleasant tone in this department and most of the girls are attentive. - The presence of three classes in an undivided main room is inconvenient. The Head teacher has introduced Brush drawing and some Morris dances. Dictionaries are needed for the 1st Class."

Death of King Edward VII

Owing to the death of King Edward VII on May 6th the Annual Prize Distribution did not take place at the Town Hall, it was conducted instead at the school by Mrs. **S. H. Addenbrooke**. "The teachers and children sent a laurel chaplet to Windsor on the occasion of the funeral of His Late Majesty." The annual treat had to be postponed.

In June Mrs. Rogers reported: "The vicar - Rev. J. F. Kershaw called in the afternoon to say "Goodbye" to the Teachers and Scholars as he is leaving the parish after 28 years residence. He built this school".

A visit to Chlidema

In January 1911 the children of the 4th Standard had a lesson on the **Manufacture of Carpets** and in the afternoon a number of them accompanied by Miss Barker visited Chlidema Carpet Works and had the process explained to them.

In February the **Inspector** noted:

> "No entries in Summary Register subsequently to January 31st. The required entries should be made at the end of each week. Regulation 28. In Standard I there are **64 children** on the Register under the instruction of one teacher."

New dual desks

In March the long awaited new dual desks arrived, 15 in number but they had to be added to ends of the rows of long desks in the large room in order to avoid using a side desk and so getting an "unsuitable view of the Blackboard." The classes were organised in rows around the room, each facing a wall.

Coronation of King George V

In May it was reported: "The King having expressed a desire that the Elementary School Children should have a weeks holiday for the Coronation, the usual Whit- holiday would be shortened to the Monday and Tuesday only." This was later changed and one week was allowed for each event. (The schools would lose the fees for holiday weeks.)

In June all the children rehearsed their songs at Brinton Park that they were to sing at the Coronation Festivities. On the 21st they rehearsed with other schools at the Shrubbery. When the great day came on the 22nd they were entertained to tea and then marched to the Town Hall where they joined a united procession of the various schools and proceeded to the Park. Here they sang the National Anthem, Land of Hope and Glory, O God our Help and Rule Britannia. The teachers were also entertained to tea at the Park. Each child received a commemorative medal of the Crowning of King George and Queen Mary.

Two days later Mrs. Baynes of Summer Hill House [Bewdley Hill] invited all St. John's school children to her residence where they had refreshments and were each presented with a Foley China Mug as a souvenir of the Coronation.

Coronation Mugs presented at St. John's Boy's School   Courtesy of Gil Edwards

Parents invited to school

In July there appears to have been a new innovation when the parents were invited to visit the school to see the children at work and to inspect an "Exhibition of Drawing and other School Work".

The Vicar called one day in August to say that the Managers had bought the adjoining house and garden to increase the size of the playground. This was more than necessary since there were now **309** girls on the books.

Housewifery at Caldwell Hall

November saw the start of the Housewifery courses at Caldwell Hall. 18 girls started a continuous course lasting three weeks.

The teachers and girls responded to the **Titanic Disaster** by sending 32 shillings to the fund in April **1912.**

A Brook Street Class   Courtesy of Gil Edwards

An eclipse of the Sun

Later in the same month Mrs Rogers lectured all the school upon the Eclipse of the Sun, they were able to view it at playtime and between 11-12 a.m., the children were sent out in batches to view it with smoked glass or pails of water. At the end of that month 60 girls went to Malvern to compete in Class 1 of the Worcestershire Musical Competition. Their test piece "Winds are blowing" gained them 75 marks, the highest mark was 76.

June was marked by the delivery of two easels in place of the two Black Board stands that had supplemented the easels at the time of the inventory in **1903**.
In a follow up to the parents day in the previous year there was a 'Mothers' day' when parents were invited not only to an exhibition of schoolwork, but also to an entertainment and tea.

A Student Teacher

At the end of August a new 'Student Teacher' is mentioned who was observing the 4th Standard for a week before taking responsibility. This appears to have been a new departure in the method of teacher training.

40 girls went to Birmingham in May to sing in the Midland Musical Competition.

Swimming

In July three girls who were competing for the Schools Shield were allowed to go swimming in the Reservoir on Thursdays, it was the only day ladies and girls could swim there.

A School Clinic

September saw the opening of the School Clinic on Prospect Hill. It was also the month when the school was too full to accommodate any Poor Law pupils (from the Union Workhouse). They were admitted to Bennett Street School instead. On Empire Day, May 22, **1914** the girls marched around Summer Green singing patriotic songs. (In front of Summer Place.)

In June Miss **N. K. Wellings** was appointed Head Mistress of Lea Street Girl's School. Mrs. Rogers wrote: "She has been a most exemplary Head Assistant in every way during the last seven years."

The same month **Vaughan Williams** gave a most favourable criticism of the girls singing at Malvern.

Outbreak of War
The outbreak of war prompted the Head to give the children an address upon the European war and its causes. In September she sent a long list of children whose parents required relief "during the present distress". She wrote two weeks later that some children were having free breakfasts and dinners owing to the European War.

Trafalgar Day
On Trafalgar Day in October Mrs. Rogers showed the children a 'Times' newspaper of 1805 containing news of the Victory of Trafalgar and Collingwood's Dispatches. Later in the month she wrote "The girls have knitted 30 pairs of socks and a lot of mittens for Soldiers and Sailors. These have given great satisfaction and Colonel Watson has asked if they can give more." In June of **1915** two baskets of eggs were collected for the wounded soldiers at **The Larches.**

Absence for confinements
The Head wrote in regard to attendance: "Each girl expects and generally has a fortnight's absence for the mothers, and sometimes another relatives Confinement. The effect this slackness of attendance has upon the children is one of indifference to education."

France's Day
During **WWI** 'France's Day' was celebrated on the 14th of July, in **1915** the children were given a half-holiday and taken in procession through the town to the Town Hall and then to Brinton Park, there they were addressed by the Mayor and saluted the French Flag. In the same month Nature Study expeditions were organised by Mrs. Rogers.

Shorthand and French
The entry in the Log Book for January 24 **1916** reads: "As a good number of girls are now being employed in the local works, offices and shops as clerks, a weekly lesson is given to the First Class girls in Shorthand and French."

Zepplins
In February the Mistress wrote "A good number of girls absent because of nervousness from last nights Zeppelin Scare".
The girls were continuing to send socks, mufflers and mittens to the soldiers and sailors and were contributing to the Red Cross, Serbian funds and to the British and Foreign Sailors Society. Their education was still being hindered by outbreaks of measles.

The clocks had to be altered in May when the **Daylight Saving Bill** came in for the first time.

Empire Day became even more important. "The girls assembled as usual and after Prayers were addressed by the Head Mistress on the Empire, the Colonies and the loyalty of the troops from all parts. They afterwards sang 'The Flag Song', and saluted the 'Union Jack'. They then marched in procession to the adjoining Green [at Summer Place] where they sang patriotic songs and the National songs of the different Allies. At 10.50 a.m. after cheers for the King and troops they were dismissed for the day."

1917 began with a cold spell and even in March the temperature was 37o and they had no coke, the children were sent home until the afternoon on the 8th, this was followed by a severe snowstorm on the 23rd. The attendance was low with the weather conditions and another outbreak of measles.

Potato and Bread shortages
In May several girls were coming in late having had to stand in queues for potatoes. Children were being discouraged from bringing large quantities of bread for their lunches and lessons were being given on economy and substitutes for wheat flour. The annual tea party could not be given because of bread and sugar problems.

In June the Head Mistress "took the 7th Standard girls for a Nature Walk, through Stone Finney to **Harvington Hall**, an old Tudor mansion about 5 miles distant. The various historical points of interest were pointed out. The children collected specimens of grasses and flowers, which they named on their return to school the next day. They had tea at Harvington and returned back at 7.15 p.m." Quite a full day!
Harvington Hall had been bought and renovated by the Roman Catholic Authorities, and was no longer a ruin.

In September **1917** Mrs. Rogers was writing about the need for Commercial teaching, she said that for over a year Miss Wridgway taught shorthand but that the present staff did not allow the time, the classes at the Technical School were only held in the evening, too late for young children.

The girls had collected nearly half a ton of horse chestnuts for the Government, they were used in the making of explosives.

January **1918** contained a half-holiday for good attendance, there had been no recent epidemics, this state continued for some time, though the school roll was falling with families moving out of the town to 'Munitions Areas'. Families replacing them were for some reason without children.

Food Rationing
School closed early one day in February for the staff to meet the representatives of The Local Food Control Committee with regard to making arrangements for the registration of the townspeople for a rationing scheme. At the beginning of March the teachers managed to register the local families, though four teachers were absent at that time. At the end of the month, the attendance at school was very considerably affected by children staying away to stand in queues at food shops.
May, then as now was found to be an ideal time for **pond dipping**. The top three Standards were taken for a spring nature walk and came back with "some fine specimens of newts, water whelks, water beetles etc. and returned about 6 p.m."

Teachers' Salaries raised
At the end of May, rather surprisingly, teachers' salaries were revised and raised "according to a new Scheme or Scale". Perhaps it reflected wartime inflation.

There was a half-holiday for a Social gathering in July. The girls performed a Dramatic Sketch written by the Mistress called *The Passing of War*.

Another Brook Street Class   Courtesy of Gil Edwards

Spanish Flu

On the 8th day of July the entry "Miss Parsons away - Influenza." heralded the coming epidemic that was known then as 'Spanish Flu' and was to sweep through Europe killing a devastating number of people in its wake. On the 9th Mrs. Johnson did not return at noon, and by the 12th attendance had fallen to 65%. The Education Authority closed the school on the 17th of July until August the 26th. It was closed again in October, when it re-opened in November the attendance had fallen to 71%.

Armistice

The Log Book doesn't mention the Armistice that took place on **November 11th** as the schools were closed from the 23rd of October until November 18th, 66 girls were still absent then.

In January **1919** a 'Victory Christmas Party' was held. There had been no parties during the war and Mrs. Rogers thought that the girls had worked so hard for 'National Causes' that they deserved one then. Over £100 and gifts in kind had been subscribed for the party.

Late Peace Festivities

The Peace Festivities took place on July 19th **1919**: "The children were entertained to tea, and afterwards marched to the Municipal Buildings where with all the other elementary schools they sang, From *East to West*, *Land of our Birth*, *There's a Land* and the National Anthem. Afterwards they proceeded to the Brinton Park, but the heavy rain prevented the Sports from taking place, and the performance of a Sketch and Recital by the Girls of this School was also postponed." This was sad when they had waited so long for the event.

In October the top class were taken to **St. Mary's Church** for a history lesson by the Head Mistress. "They took down historical notes and had the various points of interest shown to them, the choice of such a site, the early history of the surrounding country, Danish Invasion etc."

The school observed the first anniversary of the Armistice on **November 11th**.

A Sewing Machine

Later in the month the Education Committee supplied the school with a sewing machine. "With this addition to the school apparatus more time can be devoted to the mending of garments", wrote Mrs. Rogers. The girls already learnt various branches of dressmaking including pattern making.

Ballroom dancing

The Log Book entry for the 30th January **1920**: " The girls had their annual party in the Institute in Crowther Street from 6-0 p.m. They are taught the ordinary ballroom dances after school hours. A large number of parents attended."

Burnham Scale of salaries adopted

On the 30th of April the Mistress reported: "The Local Education Authority has adopted the Burnham Scale of Salaries and the teachers today receive the addition to their usual monthly amounts." At the same time she reported that she had made alterations in the timetable to enable the children to benefit from "any individual teacher's special qualifications." Some of the teachers were regular attendants at the School of Art.

In June Mrs. Rogers received a circular from the Head Mistress of the local High School stating that the County Council would be prepared to receive several 'well recommended' girls who would eventually be trained as teachers.

Aid from the U.S.A.

In 1921 "Doris Whittall was recommended for a scholarship at the High School but was medically disqualified as unfit to eventually take up school teaching as a profession. The head mistress "acquainted **Matthew Whittall** of Worcester, Mass: USA, a wealthy Carpet Manufacturer, and after correspondence he has generously forwarded a draft of Fifty two pounds to the High School Authorities for her education to the age of sixteen."

A weekly debate was instituted; the girls of the first class were stimulated by such propositions as "Should we abolish examinations?" An entry in December reads: "In order to emphasize History, all lessons to be dramatised- notes to be written by the teacher assisted by the Class ---." Christmas entertainment was provided for by items from all of the classes, they included ambitious presentations such as "Aladdin" and scenes from Shakespeare.

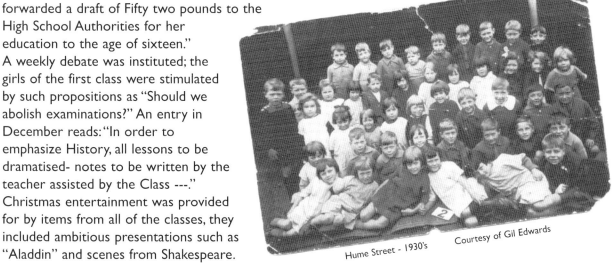

Hume Street - 1930's

Courtesy of Gil Edwards

An extract from the **Inspector's Report** for 1922 reads:

> "The headmistress is devoted to her work and is unsparing in her efforts for the welfare of her girls; she has attracted a body of conscientious assistants to help her."

School Visits

In July of that year the top two Standards went to Redstone Caves near Stourport to see the hermitage of Layamon, writer of The Brut. They had previously had lessons on the Arthurian Poets.

Malvern Sanatorium

It was usual for three girls to be chosen to attend the Malvern Sanatorium for a period of three months to improve their health. The Mistress wrote that when they returned: "They have gained very considerably in weight and height."

An official notice was received on April 26 1923 which read: "By the command of His Majesty the King a whole holiday is to be given on the occasion of the marriage of the **Duke of York and Lady Elizabeth Bowes-Lyon**." These occasional Holidays must have boosted the popularity of the Royals!

Measles again

Attendance was reduced at this time owing to an epidemic of Measles. Miss Parsons was absent for ten weeks in total suffering from rheumatism following on measles. This entailed the Mistress taking her 3rd Standard as well as her own 7th Standard. She wrote: "Considerable difficulty has been experienced in testing the work this term". Her normal complement of staff was five teachers (three uncertificated) for eight Standards. Seven and Eight were taught together because 'Standard*' was a diminishing class with girls leaving as they reached their 14th birthday. In July the Public Vaccinator vaccinated 80 children because of an outbreak of Smallpox at Gloucester.

In August Eileen Tipper, not yet eighteen years of age, was the replacement for a member of staff who had left. She was paid as a Monitress until she was eighteen. She had taken examinations equivalent to Matriculation. The mistress wrote: "Ten recently admitted girls from various schools are quite unable to read. Delicate health and general dullness seem to be the cause of this backward state."

The girls went on various **Nature expeditions** in September. The 7th Standard visited Arley Church. Rock Church was the original place of visit but at the last moment the bus was too crowded to carry more than six.

In early October Mrs. Rogers reports: "Miss Tipper is making progress under the close supervision of the Head for one week then she has alternate weeks in a separate room in order that she may gain confidence."

Collapse of Mrs. Rogers

By October 15th the Head Mistress was away ill. On October 22nd the Log Book entry read: "Head Mistress still away Complete Collapse." On November 5th Mrs. **Linecar** formerly Head Mistress of Bennett St. Infants School, was sent to assist during her absence. Mrs. Rogers was away until the 14th of December.

She appears to have completely recovered her energy the next year as the entry for July 22nd **1924** shows: "The whole school has been examined in each subject by the Head Mistress." This continued to be Lucy Rogers' method of getting results, she had begun that way in 1893 (this task appears to have been expected of Mistresses from the early days) and continued it though the numbers on roll were more than 200.

On September 5th she wrote "Ten girls who are visiting the **Wembley Exhibition** on Monday and Tuesday next week are being medically examined by Dr. Griffiths at the clinic tomorrow. This is necessary as they will sleep at a Hostel and the Ministry of Health require such precaution." Mrs. Rogers accompanied the girls to Wembley.

Again she shows her control of affairs when she writes on December 12th "All examinations complete, subjects discussed with the Head Mistress, weaknesses pointed out and suggestions for improvement recommended. The children have received their term reports which they have taken home."

In **1925** the year started with a lot of sickness including mumps and influenza, attendance fell to 77.4% in March. The 7th Standard were busy acting three scenes from the "Merchant of Venice" to the rest of the school, the Head Mistress supplying the connecting links.

The L.E.A. now required the children to observe Empire Day in the latter part of the day. They sang their usual songs and were addressed by the Head and then marched to the Memorial Cross in the churchyard where they sang Kipling's 'Recessional' etc.

The Cross had previously been cleaned and decorated by the Head Mistress and the older girls.

Infants transferred to Hume Street
In October the Infants were transferred to the more modern building of Hume Street School, belonging to the Local Education Authority, as the old Infant's school in Chapel Street had been condemned as unsuitable.

Christmas concert
In December the girls held their Christmas Concert and Entertainment at the Conservative Club Room. Each child took part, each class performing sketches, the 1ˢᵗ Class, Dickens Christmas Carols and three scenes from the Merchant of Venice. They repeated their Christmas Concert at the Town Hall in February.

1926 started with severe weather and measles again, with consequently poor attendance. In March an entertainment was given at the close of school and the proceeds forwarded to Stratford on Avon towards the rebuilding of the **Shakespeare Memorial Theatre.**

Mrs. Rogers resigns
The Log Book entry for April 10ᵗʰ reads:

> *"I resign my post as Head Mistress of this school, having held the appointment since June 12 1893.*
> *Lucy A. Rogers. L.L.A.*

Her resignation took place two and a half years after her original collapse. **Nellie Kate Wellings** took over the headship on April 12ᵗʰ. She was a former pupil and Pupil Teacher at St. John's, as the latter she had gained a 1ˢᵗ in the Scripture examinations in 1904 and was appointed Head Teacher to Lea Street School in 1914.

Inspector's report
It would appear from the **H.M.I.s** report that Lucy Rogers had suffered another breakdown, for he wrote in October:

> "The Top Class is well taught and the girls are making satisfactory progress. In the other classes the work has deteriorated since the last visit of inspection, especially that of Standard V where the work is disappointing in the extreme. This is due to the illness of the late Head Mistress, the frequent changes of teachers, and the appointment of inexperienced assistants. The new Head Mistress, who took charge in April last, is making strenuous efforts to raise the school to its former level, but with the Staff as at present constituted this is an almost impossible task."

Prior to the illness of Mrs. Rogers there had been a succession of resignations on the part of the teachers, through marriage, promotion, illness and removal. It is not difficult to account for her breakdown.

However since her appointment in 1893 until her collapse in 1923 Lucy Rogers had obviously been of very great benefit to the school. Girls were given opportunities both social and in learning that were not usually available in Church and Board schools. She also played her part in the educational affairs of the town, her school was looked to as an example of good practise. She had had the advantage of not taking on the responsibility of the school straight from college, as her predecessors had done. She had evidently taught in the town prior to her appointment to St. John's, the 1891 Census shows her living at 11 Chester Road and described as 'School Mistress'.

She was born in Broseley to Josiah and Susannah Wase. Josiah was born in Kidderminster. He was shown as a 'Roofing Tile Maker'on the Census of 1871 when Lucy was 5. She was the fifth of six children, three older siblings aged 10 18 years old were already tile makers like their father. Ten years later, still in Broseley she was listed as 'Pupil Teacher, National School'. In Kidderminster she married Thomas James Rogers who was a Rate Collector in 1901, at that time they lived at Brookfield, near to 61 Bewdley Street, now in the hospital grounds. Lucy's mother-in-law and a general servant were part of the household. A son, George, had been born in 1892/3 and daughters Mary and Barbara in 1895/6 and 1900. It's hard to detect from the Log Book when she was confined. She was absent for a week in 1895 and appears to have had her second daughter in the Whitsun holiday in 1900 since she was 10 months old at the time of the 1901 Census.

Miss Wellings continued to provide activities for the girls. In July some were taken to the Domestic Centre Ground to learn to play basketball. Mrs. Rogers had been one of a committee involved in developing the new sports grounds at Caldwell Hall. The same month the children lined the route when the **Duke of York** (later George VI) opened the new wing to Kidderminster Hospital. In October the top Standards were taken to the theatre to witness *The Tempest*.

1927 started with an outbreak of Influenza, by February the attendance was down to 60%, the school was ordered to close for a fortnight. To make matters worse the heating was not working properly. By the end of March no fires could be made while repairs were done. The **H.M.I.** visited the school in May. As Mrs. Griffiths was in charge of 60 girls (Standards 6 &7) he wished ten to work with Standard 5. He asked what steps were being taken to strengthen the Staff. In July Miss Marjorie Rawlings, a trained teacher with two years experience, was appointed in place of the inexperienced Miss Morgan who had joined the staff the previous summer and had now left.

Two girls were reported to have died in October, one from Scalds and one from Rheumatic Fever, it made the girls very sad.

In March **1928** 40 senior girls attended a lecture on Canada at the Town Hall arranged by the Education Committee and illustrated by **lantern slides**
.

Unsuitable desks
In April Mr. Sandys the **H.M.I.** called to see if any new desks had been supplied since he reported on them over 2 years ago. He called again in July and commented again upon the unsuitability of the desks now in use. In October the newly appointed Chairman of the Education Committee, Mr. **Harry Cheshire** visited the school with Mr. **Roden**. The antiquated desks were again commented upon. It took another six months for **20 new dual desks** (locker type) to be delivered.

21 girls went to **Windsor** in July that year accompanied by Miss Wellings and Mrs. Griffiths. They were conducted over the grounds of the castle and St. George's Chapel, spending the afternoon on a trip to Runnymede Island.
In November the Town Council invited one senior scholar from each school to attend the Mayor-making meeting.

Large Classes
In April **1930** classes had to be arranged so as to keep the numbers in Standards III & IV down to 50.

In June the school was closed to allow some of the children to go to **London**, the trip had been arranged by the local teachers and the Chairman of the Education Committee paid for one child from each department to go.

In **1931** attendance was very low in March through influenza and colds, added to by cases of measles and whooping cough. Attendance for the 2nd week was down to 80%.

In March **25 new locker desks** were delivered. In April there were 252 girls on the books, and an additional teacher was promised. Miss Barth was appointed who was both <u>Trained</u> and Certificated. (There was a difference.)

Fourteen children visited **Hampton Court** and **Kew Gardens** at the end of June.

The Log Book entry for July 31st records: "Attendance has been poor throughout the week but this morning only 219 are present out of 262, many have started on holiday this morning as parents take advantage of **excursion trains**."

Disarmament
On **Remembrance Day** the mistress spoke about the importance of the forthcoming Geneva Conference on Disarmament.

The report for November 30th "Owing to Reorganisation the children from **Foley Park Mixed School** have had to leave if [they are] 11+ years. All who applied for admission here could not be accepted because classes were already full. Nine have been accepted."

In **1932** the Head explained to Miss Pountney the Inspector, the difficulty she would have in accommodating new scholars in April, as there were already 274 girls on the books.

In March the Vicar presented prizes and certificates to the girls as usual. He also gave a silver cross to the girl considered by the others to have the best character. Voting for this had been done on the previous day and the recipient was **Pearl Marsh**.

The girls now went to the **Larches Playing Field** for their Basket Ball. The new Domestic Centre was opened in April.

Staff and scholars buy a piano
Also in April a second-hand Challen piano and trolley was delivered. The Staff and scholars had been raising money in small sums for six years to buy the better piano.

In June the Top Class played Basket Ball on the new court made at **Caldwell**.

In July 38 pupils went to London by train with three staff. They were to visit the Tower and the Zoo.

Staff raise money for Electric Lighting
During the summer holiday, electric lighting was installed. The Staff had raised the money for the lighting excepting for a £5 grant from the Education Committee. The total cost was £20-13-9d. The Managers managed to find the money for three new basins for the cloakroom the next year.

1933 Under the headship of Miss Wellings the children continued to gain Art Scholarships and prizes in out of school competitions for Art and other competitions. She continued Mrs. Roger's method in examining the children throughout the school.

Class of 86
In May Miss Wellings was obliged to take two classes together numbering 86 in the absence for two days of Miss Hayward with a swollen face from a tooth extraction.

Swimming success
In September there was a Swimming Gala for the Elementary Schools of the town, held in the new Swimming Baths in Castle Street. St. John's Girls won the Shield.
In October the Mistress reported that attendance had been very poor with Mumps, Chicken Pox, Measles and Fever prevalent besides general sickness. Soon after that came the report of the death of Muriel Tranter from the top class from Pneumonia, she had been operated upon in hospital but died a few weeks later.

The **H.M.I.s report** in October stated that the school continued to do good work but pointed out:

> "[The] uniformity of results is attained in each class partly by promotion of the quick workers and keeping down the slower children, so that there is in general too wide an age-range in classes." Miss Pountney went on to say that" if the teachers could break away with tradition and do more sectional work in their classes the slower children would benefit considerably. The very cramped conditions, which unfortunately must continue until reorganisation of the schools is made, no doubt makes sectional teaching unusually difficult, but it is felt that something should be done to give slow children a better chance to reach the upper school."

1934 began with much illness and the death of another pupil. The head succumbed to Influenza herself in February.

In April, the School Managers provided a small cycle shelter as so many children cycled to school.

The **H.M.I.** called in May and expressed his willingness to give another teacher if there was another classroom.

Halfpenny milk
October the 1st brought a letter to say that the children could now have a third of a pint of milk for a halfpenny. November brought cases of (Scarlet) Fever again.

1935 started with cases of Diphtheria, Miss Edwards, one of the teachers succumbed to it, as well as several children. The school was closed for two weeks, as other cases were reported. Two girls died from diphtheria, another from pneumonia. Miss Edwards returned in March having been absent for two months.

Silver Jubilee of King George V
After the sadness came the celebrations for the Jubilee of King George V in May.
A holiday was granted for the 6th and 7th and the Staff and 'big girls' spent the whole of Saturday morning until 1-30 p.m. decorating the school in readiness for the Jubilee Party. On May 6th all teachers spent the whole morning preparing for the tea. A sum of 9d per head was allowed so it was considered that a good tea was possible.

"Just before children took their places, the Mayor (Mr. A. Meredith), his wife, and daughter, came to the School. Following them were Councillor Cheshire (Chairman of the Education Committee) and Councillor O. Davis. Mistress quickly assembled the scholars in the Playground where the Mayor addressed them upon the importance of the occasion. In addition to the tea each scholar at this School had a Souvenir Tin filled with Cadbury's Chocolate as Mistress thought this a "better way of spending some of the money, than letting it all go on cakes."

"After the tea the children were conducted to Brinton Park where entertainments of all kinds were provided. These were thoroughly enjoyed, as weather was perfect. A firework display ended the proceedings. The Town Council provided each child with a souvenir mug in addition to the tea."

The Town Council were evidently feeling the pinch after all the expenditure for the Jubilee, for a note was received in July stating that: "the Finance Committee could not sanction the consumption of gas for other than lighting purposes." The Head Teacher forwarded this letter to the Vicar, who, later on, called in to say that he had "asked the Gas Company to send the bill to the Managers. Apparently the Finance committee do not intend to provide facilities for getting hot drinks for children who stay at school for mid-day break." (The H.M.I. had earlier encouraged the school to supply plates and tablecloths and hot drinks when it was cold, for the dinner break.)

Staff hire Wireless Set
The Log Book entry for January 22nd **1936** records:

"The staff hired a Wireless Set for today to enable the children to hear the **Proclamation of King Edward VIII**. As two special talks to the children, lasting 20 minutes each, were broadcast in the afternoon, the Head teacher allowed Standards 4,5,6 and 7 to rearrange lessons and listen to them. During the first 20 minutes Mr. **Owen Morshead**, the King's Librarian, and Sir **Walford Davies**, Master of the King's Musick spoke of various visits they had paid to the King and his talks with them, the former referring to his last visit only a week before when the King rode his favourite pony Jock. Sir Walford Davies made known that "Jerusalem" was one of the King's favourite hymns. The second talk was by Commander **Stephen King-Hall** whose topic was "The King and his people". He too was able to relate conversations he had held with his late Majesty King George V.

On January 23rd "At 11-30 Head Teacher with Girl Guides and the top class left school in order to attend the **proclamation of King Edward VIII**. A letter requesting their presence at the Ceremony had been received. The proclamation was made by **Miss Addenbrooke** the first lady Mayor of the Borough."

The school was closed the next day, the day that **King George V** was to be buried at Windsor after his 'Lying in State' at Westminster Hall.

Staff shortage
In February the Head reported: "For a second week the school has been carried on under great difficulties. When large classes have no teacher, it is impossible for work to go forward as it should." One teacher had been sent on an arts course and another had German Measles. In July the **Inspector** called to check the registers, she found them correct, and added "Have also listened to some delightful singing, the choice of songs and the way they were rendered were really admirable." It would seem that the high standard of singing nurtured by Mrs. Rogers had continued into another generation.

Class of Ninety

In November Rev. Noel Panter, Diocesan Inspector noted "For Scripture Lessons some of the classes are unduly large. Is 90 children a suitable number for one teacher? N.B. The quality of the teaching and discipline is excellent."

Log Book entry for May 3rd 1937: "Framed photographs of the new King and Queen, King George VI, and Queen Elizabeth were received today from the Education Committee."

Coronation of King George VI and Queen Elizabeth

On the 11th of May the children had a service in the church in commemoration of the Coronation. The next day a tea was given to all the children. The Mayor, E. G. Eddy presented the children with a Coronation Mug, after which the children were taken to the Park and entertained by Concert Parties. Sports were also held, three of the girls won prizes.

Money raised to buy sewing machine

Other special news was reported on June 1st "By various efforts the money to purchase an additional sewing machine has been raised. This is a hand machine (Singer) and its cover is an attaché case. One sewing machine in a school of this size has been found to be quite inadequate."

One of the six children awarded Special Places at the Girl's High School at that time was **Marjorie Samuel** (now Sykes), her selection for the special place resulted in a long teaching career. The girls who were selected as being suitable, as well as sitting an examination went for an interview with Miss Oldfield, the Headmistress of the High School, Marjorie was asked to describe something in her daily life, she remembers talking about the bank of daffodils in Lowe Lane and was awarded a place. She had been admitted from South Wales in the January and says that she had not found the work of the school demanding. Remembering the school and Miss Wellings she says that it was a happy place, though Miss Wellings was something of a martinet. She says that they had some of the **long six-seater desks** even then. **Beryl Gaston** remembers the knitted suits that she wore.

In October an outbreak of Scarlet Fever caused the school to be closed for a fortnight.

King George Playing Field

In May 1938 the Mayor opened the King George playing field, given by **Mr. Gerald Tomkinson** to mark the Coronation. Later that month 99 girls visited Dudley Zoo, travelling there in three charabancs.

Air Raid Precautions

On 28th September the following communication was received:

> "The Air Raid Precaution Committee have considered the question of dealing with children in the case of an Emergency and in all probability according to Government information, schools would be closed down for one month immediately an emergency arises. The school will be used for about one evening a week for the fitting and issue of gas masks."

Four Power Pact

On Sept. 30th Miss Wellings writes: "Better news is announced in daily papers. Mr. Neville Chamberlain, our Prime Minister, Herr Hitler, Signor Mussolini and the French Prime Minister have entered into a Four Power Pact regarding settlement in Sudetan territory."

In **1939** the year opened with severe weather and fresh cases of mumps. Later in the year the girls were to keep up their high standard for singing at the Festival. In July, in line with the schools' reputation for swimming, the Cup for the best swimmer in the town was presented to Joan Smith, though St. Mary's won the Shield.

It was announced that the Act for the new **school leaving age of 15** years was to come into force on September 1ˢᵗ **1939**.

As the school broke up for the summer holiday, holiday addresses of the Staff were sent to the Education office in order that they could be recalled should a national emergency arise.

Outbreak of World War II

On September 3ʳᵈ war was declared, the school re-opened on the 11ᵗʰ after being closed for an extra weeks holiday on account of the national situation. Teachers were recalled to complete arrangements for billeting children of school age, and mothers and babies from Smethwick. Only 80 came instead of the 200 that had been expected. By the 26ᵗʰ excavations to make an air-raid shelter under the school had been commenced. The Head Mistress queried the direction of the Chairman of the Education Committee that all children should remain in school unless called for by parents, she thought that such a ruling was not in the best interests of the children unless sufficient air raid shelter could be provided for all.

On November 20ᵗʰ the order was given: "Beginning today the afternoon session is to end at 3-30 p.m. to enable the children to reach home before dark as there is **no street lighting**." The Christmas tea party could not be held because the children would have to leave at 3-30 p.m.

January **1940** started with the beginning of a very memorable cold winter. By the 29ᵗʰ of January only 91 out of 254 children were present at school. The air-raid shelters were completed by the end of February.

Help for Finnish children

A collection was made for the relief of Finnish children affected by the war. In May a collection was made in aid of the Over Seas Tobacco Fund and £2-10-0s was forwarded.

The Whitsuntide holiday was interrupted by a Radio Message from the Government, all schools were to resume work to enable evacuation schemes to take effect should necessity arise, because **Germany had invaded Holland and Belgium** on May 10ᵗʰ.

Billeting evacuees

On the 30ᵗʰ of May the school was closed to enable the teachers to arrange billets for children who were to be evacuated from the S.E. coast. These children were to reach Kidderminster on Sunday June 2ⁿᵈ. On June 3ʳᵈ "News came from the Ministry of Health that **children would not be sent here**." This came on Friday evening after the canvass had been made so householders had to be informed of this on Saturday.

Leaving age continues to be 14

The raising of the school age to 15 had been put aside, children reaching the age of 14 could now leave without staying on to the end of the term. Twenty-five girls left the school in one week as a result of the ruling.

Children were losing hours of sleep because air-raid sirens were sounded and the 'all-clear' was often only sounded 6 hours later. German aircraft were flying over Kidderminster en route to bomb Birmingham.

Senior Schools

In September the Education Office was asking for a list of Teachers wishing to teach in Senior Schools and the subjects in which they were qualified to specialize. (Kidderminster schools were 'all age' schools until **Harry Cheshire** and **Sladen Schools** were built.) The Senior Schools were to be opened on October 1st. Furniture would be collected from schools at the weekend. Three members of staff were told that they were to teach at **Habberley Road Girls' School.**

Visits to the shelter

On October 1st only 3 classes remained, numbering 109 children. 144 had gone to Habberley Road and Sladen schools. During that month there were many visits to the shelter, sometimes as many a three in a day.

January **1941** was dark and cold. Because of the continuance of Summer Time throughout the winter months, blackboard and bookwork were impossible early in the day. (Lights could not be shown, windows had to be blacked out and criss-crossed with brown sticky paper to protect them in case of explosion tremors). Snow fell heavily later in the month and children were sent home. The roads were in "a shocking state".

In February Miss Wellings wrote: "The **sewing machine** supplied to this school by the Committee many years ago [in 1919] has been sent to the new Senior School at Habberley Rd."

Bungalow and School bombed

On May 19th Miss Wellings reported: "Children had much to say concerning the Air Raid on Friday evening or rather 1 a.m. Saturday May 17th. Many of them lived quite near to the bungalow that was demolished and to houses that suffered. Some of their houses lost glass etc. The new school in Habberley Road received several direct hits so it will be some time before it can be used."

Warships Week

In December the morning session began at 9-30 a.m. to prevent pupils starting from their homes in 'Black Out' time. The next week was "Warships Week" in Kidderminster, when it was hoped to raise £210,000. A van for showing pictures of aircraft was stationed at the school for the children to see the pictures to encourage them to save for the war effort. They were asked to submit posters showing the need to salvage all waste materials. Since these were to be done at home only three entered the competition!

Teachers wash up

A Log Book entry for March **1942** noted: "School milk is now to be delivered in bulk as Dairymen can no longer fill and wash bottles because of labour shortage. Distribution and bottle washing, will in future, be done by Staff."! The same month the school windows were measured for blacking out with curtains, this was to make it possible to use lighting on the dark afternoons.

In July the school closed a week earlier than usual for the summer break so that the children could participate in the **"Holiday at Home"** scheme and enjoy the activities that were arranged in the park for the benefit of residents.

In February **1943** the Log book entry reads: " crockery to be used when school dinners are served, was delivered. Sink, draining board and water heater have been fixed in readiness." However it was not until December that the school dinners were served there for the first time. A cloakroom had been fitted up as a kitchen and the caretaker appointed to serve the meals and to wash-up afterwards. The meals were brought by 'motor-van' from the Schools' Food Centre in Coventry Street. Children paid two shillings and sixpence for five dinners. 36 children were present the first day when the Head and two of the staff supervised, but it was hoped that two would be enough later. (It helped to eke out the meat ration if children had dinner at school.)

In May **1944** Empire Day was still observed, but now the children "stopped ordinary lessons to listen to the 'Empire broadcast for Schools'.

In August three evacuees from the South were admitted, "where **flying bombs** have caused such havoc". Gas masks were regularly checked for leaks, children were usually in trouble if they forgot to bring them, though fortunately they were never needed.

At the end of October top class children were taken to the library where an **Anglo-Soviet Exhibition** had been staged, in order to foster the Anglo-Soviet Youth Friendship Alliance.

At the end of December **Mrs. Griffiths** retired, she had been Assistant Head for nearly thirty years. Miss Wellings wrote: "She will be greatly missed for she has been an excellent teacher in every way. She had a splendid influence over all her scholars whether young or old."

In **1945** January started with snow by the end of the month there was only 42% attendance. In April the children's milk was brought in bottles again, the bottles had been washed and filled by the staff since March 1942.

Victory in Europe
On May 8th came the long awaited announcement:

> "Over the Radio last evening it was announced that May 8th was to be observed a **V.E. Day**. The Prime Minister Mr. Churchill made a formal announcement at 3 p.m. and the King spoke at 9 p.m."

The children had a holiday for that and the next day, but the Log entry doesn't give any hint of the jubilation that was felt, even though only part of the war was over. Dancing in the streets came in August and subsequent street parties when **VJ Day** (Victory in Japan) was announced. It didn't get a mention in the school records because it occurred during the summer holidays.

A nice note is struck by the entry of July 25th when the leavers before breaking up, "entertained the rest of the school with sketches, dances and songs *entirely prepared by themselves.*"

A loan to Shenstone College
An entry for May 1946 states: "A Board and Easel has been loaned to Shenstone Emergency Training College until it is equipped with its own." [Emergency Teacher Training Colleges were set up to train people leaving the forces, in 13 months.]

Recycling
On July 5th The children went to the Town Hall: "where an exhibition was staged to show the importance of saving paper, bones, tins, &c, &c. Articles made from salvage were on view, also the apparatus for pulping waste paper."

Miss Wellings retires

On November 19th Miss Wellings retired, she had held the post for over twenty years. She wrote that, "no head teacher ever had more devoted colleagues than Mrs. Griffiths (who had retired two years before) and Miss Neale" (who remained on the staff).

The **H.M.I. Report** before Miss Wellings left stated:

> "By her earnest hardworking leadership and devotion to the School, supported by her equally hardworking assistant teacher good results have been obtained. One is impressed by the quiet industry, friendliness and good behaviour of the children."

Olive Irene Jones succeeded her on December 2nd.

1947 started with **severe weather,** it was to continue into Spring. A blizzard raged all day in early March, the school managed to stay open the head wrote: "Quite an achievement in these days of fuel shortage." The war was over but there were still great shortages of fuel and goods of all kinds.

In March the staff and 70 girls paid a visit to the Playhouse to see a performance of *King Stag* played by the '**Young Vic Company'**. They enjoyed it immensely.
Miss Jones was evidently a supporter of the theatre for in October some of the girls went to the Playhouse to the 'Nonentities' performance of *The Rose without a Thorn*. Visiting shows became a regular event.

Buying a Wireless Set

In **1948** one of the mothers organised a concert held in St. John's Institute in aid of the School Radio Fund. It made a profit of £5 5 shillings. They subsequently bought a Schools Wireless Set, the Education Authority contributing half the cost.

The death of the Head Teacher

On February 14th **1949** the Log Book recorded: "The sad message of the passing of our Head Teacher (Miss Olive Irene Jones) was received by phone message yesterday (Sunday) afternoon. She had been absent since the Christmas Holidays yet her death came as a shock to us."

Miss Neale appointed new Head

Miss Neale was appointed as Head Teacher from the 1st of May.

In **1950** the school was now reported as having four classrooms, it would seem that the 'Large Room' had been divided at last. From the 9th of April **1951** the school became a '**Controlled School**".

In June over a 100 girls went on a coach tour to Warwick, Leamington and Stratford-on-Avon.

The new school year in September opened with 180 girls on the books, 27 were admitted as a temporary arrangement from the new Birchen Coppice estate (45 per classroom). This caused difficulties in serving dinners, tables were not able to be used as there were so many desks in the room.

The death of King George VI
On the 12th of February **1952** there was a short memorial service "for our beloved King George the Sixth who died suddenly in his sleep on the 6th February."

In March the long awaited **school badges** arrived, to be worn by the girls and the boys of St. John's Schools. Also over 150 children and adults went on an outing to Cheltenham and the Cotswolds.

The **Birchen Coppice School** opened on 7th October, the 37 children who lived on the estate were transferred there.

Telephone installed
On the 11th of November a telephone with an extension to the Boys' and Infants' Departments was installed.

Coronation of Queen Elizabeth II
This took place on 4th June **1953**.
"School reassembled today after the Whitsun and Coronation holiday. Many children saw the Coronation Procession and the crowning of our Elizabeth II on television sets. Some have already been to 'street' parties and have received lovely Coronation Souvenirs."

On the17[th] June "Girls in classes 3,4 and 5, accompanied by their Teachers went to see a dress rehearsal performance of Shakespeare's *A Midsummer Nights Dream* at Harry Cheshire Girls' School this afternoon at **Miss Waters**, the Headmistress's kind invitation."

Mr. Benoy, the County Music Adviser was even more than usually enthusiastic about the singing of the school choir and of the verse speaking at the **1955** Music Festival. Some of the girls took part in the Children's Concerts for the **Centenary Celebrations** at the **Town Hall** in October.

The school continued in much the same manner, the choir being complimented at the annual Musical Festivals by Mr. Benoy, obtaining a fair number of places in the Girls' High School each year, visiting a surprising number of plays and having interesting outings in the summer, and were very well regarded as a school. The school now hosted students from **Shenstone College** for their school practises.

Retirement of Miss Neale and appointment of Mr. Jack Hymas
Miss Dorothy Neale retired in July **1959** she had joined the staff way back in November 1926 as an uncertificated teacher and taken an especial interest in Religious Studies and the Arts, she was appointed Head Teacher in 1949.

When the school re-opened after the summer holiday it was to a new order. The school became a **Junior Mixed School** under the Headship of Mr. Jack Hymas. In a sense it was still two schools, because all pupils could not be accommodated in either of the present buildings. So the Brook Street building was used for the 7-9 years old children and the St. Johns Street building for the older ones, since the dinners were to be served in Brook Street, it was thought better for the older children to make the walk there in bad weather. St. John's Street building had been built for Infants in 1850, but was later used by the girls until their move to Brook Street, but then refurbished to take the boys when the infants were moved back to Chapel Street. There were 132 children on roll.

We will return to **St. John's C. E. Junior Mixed School** later when we have looked at the earlier history of St. John's Boys' School.

ST. JOHN'S BOYS' SCHOOL

The first available Log Book for the boy's school is dated **1877** but no doubt the school had previously shared many similar circumstances as those of the girls. The boys were then apparently housed in the Chapel Street School on the corner of Bewdley Street (now Road).

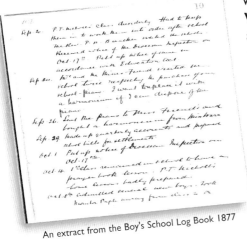

An extract from the Boy's School Log Book 1877

When the Log starts **J. Priestnall** was the Master, with **J.A. Wheeler** as Assistant, one 5th year Pupil Teacher **A. Beswick** and one 1st year Pupil Teacher **C.W.Nicholls**. Though not on the list in September P.T. Nicholls, and Monitors Chalk and Pugh are mentioned taking a class. (Harry Chalk was later sent back to his class for helping to spend stolen money.) There were 170 boys 'Qualified for Examination". The Master, together with the Girl's School Mistress was also responsible for the Evening School.

The **Inspector's Report** that year noted: "The Reading in the 1st Standard is very inferior both in care and accuracy to that of the other Standards. The rest of the work shows great care and intelligence. The order is very good."

Annual Treat

In June the Master sent back two boys to put on cleaner clothing. The same month they had their Annual Treat with a visit to Summerhill, on Bewdley Hill upon the invitation of Mr. Boyle.

School Flooded

In August the Master notes: "A tremendous fall of rain caused the floor of the school to be flooded from the drains in the yard which could not carry off the water. He "Received complaints about boys playing on the gates of the Meeting House in St. John's Terrace."

In September the Master took Standard VI and the choir-boys to the Clent Hills for an outing. They will probably have gone by train to Hagley and walked the rest of the way.

Harmonium versus piano

Mr. & Mrs. Friend came to school re the purchase of a piano, the Master wanted to replace it with a Harmonium. He bought the latter from a Miss Warr.

The **Diocesan Report** Summary stated:
 "If the lower Division was equal to the two above there would be nothing but unqualified praise to give for every branch of the Religious Instruction given in this really excellent school."

A Log Book entry for November states: "Only two lessons this afternoon as it was too dark and wet, so that it was too dirty for copy books." (At this time the lighting would have been the naked gas flame type.)

Dirty boys

In January **1878 the Master** wrote: "Two boys named Sheward were sent back to wash themselves and they have not been back since. They have been admitted to the Board School" [Hume Street]. Subsequently they returned to St. John's. (There was a "Ragged School" which would have served them marked on the 1859 map, it was not far away at the end of Park Street, it took the poorest children though it may not have been there by 1878.)

Not properly dressed
The Master reported in March:

> "Wrote a letter to the School Board respecting a boy named Barth who
> has been removed from here because I sent him back to fasten his shirt
> front and put a scarf round his neck. He has been refused admission at the
> Old Church and at the Old Meeting and has been admitted at the
> Coventry Board School."

He then:

> "Received information that the Board had decided not to admit Arthur
> Barth to their schools under the circumstances and had instructed the
> Master to refuse him when he presented himself. Barth was dismissed from
> the School Board and immediately re-admitted by the Master [of Coventry
> Street School]."

The Master complained that he acted in that way to show opposition to the other schools in
the town. Arthur Barth's father then called and made a disturbance because the boy had been
sent away from the Board School. The boy was then refused admittance to St. Ambrose
School. Both teachers and parents considered the church schools to be superior.

In May the Vicar appointed Pupil Teacher Beswick as Assistant Master. The Master constantly
complained about the work, or lack of it of P.T. Nicholls, he even copied examples of his
mistakes in the Log Book. He appeared to be trying to persuade reluctant Managers to
terminate his apprenticeship.

The Master quite often punished boys for truanting though it doesn't appear to have cured
the offence.

The **Diocesan Inspector's report** showed his pleasure with the school and its religious
instruction.

Smoking
The Master reported more trouble with Nicholls: The Pupil Teacher had sent out three boys
for punishment because they had told his mother that he had been smoking. Three boys had
been in the Back Alley, they said he had a pipe that he was lighting. He denied it, but another
boy said that he was lighting brown paper in it. The pipe belonged to another boy and they
had used it before. Subsequently Nicholls apologised both to his mother and the Master.

Gold reward
In **1879** P.T. **Beswick** entered York Training College. He was generously presented with a gold
pencil case at his departure. In February the Master reported P.T. Nicholls to the Managers
for neglecting his work and being utterly useless in school, but they took no steps to remedy
the matter.

Money for the teachers
On March 24th the Master writes:

> "Sent a boy down with a note to Mr. Woodward advising him of the
> amount necessary to pay teacher's salaries and asking him to fix a day to
> pay the same." On the 26th he again sent a boy to Mr. Woodward "asking if
> Monday [sic] as none had been sent. The boy came back and said that 'Mr.
> Woodward is surprised at you sending me down in school hours and he is
> very angry."

It seems that it was then the customary way of collecting the salaries, so he wrote courteously to Mr. Woodward pointing out how his message was calculated to do him an injury with his he was only following a practise that had existed for 8 years. Mr. Woodward wrote back denying that boys had been to his office with his knowledge

The Master wrote:
> "Mr. Woodward's letters left me with no alternative than to resign under such an affront so I have placed my resignation in the hands of the Vicar." Mr. J. Priestnall finished his tenure on May 22nd Having had it would seem, some long standing disagreements with the Vicar.

Horatio Theodore Van took charge on the 26th of May. The average attendance for May had been described as 209.6% (sic), there were obviously more than that actually on roll. However measles then struck and thinned the attendance. In June the Master wrote that he gave a lesson on '**Electric Telegraph**'. By the end of the month the attendance was now down to 145 as those with measles in the household had to stay home.

The **Inspector** noted that the school would only hold an average attendance of 189. If the rule was violated the Grant would be withheld. He further wrote:

> "**C. W. Nicholls** will not be counted on the Staff unless he can produce unqualified Managers' certificates."

The staff now comprised: The Master' an Assistant one Pupil Teacher (C.W. Nicholls) and two paid Monitors who were half-timers. On August 8th Mr Van wrote: "The Drawing Master did not come on Thursday morning so I took the whole school".

Nicholls and his misdemeanours

Nicholls was caught reading a weekly paper 'The Boys of England', while sitting with a class who had been provided with work. He was later caught reading a boy's paper to the class instead of the lesson. He graduated from brown paper to having tobacco in school. Mr. Van now pleaded with the Vicar for him to be removed, but the answer was that the father wouldn't take him away. Meanwhile one of the Monitors was in trouble for smoking. He and another were also in trouble for striking boys. The Master told the Vicar that the classes couldn't be worked properly with Monitors (they were boys from the top Standard).

In **1881** the Inspector reported: "The Boys are orderly, but not very tidy. Lavatory accommodation should be provided so as to ensure an improvement in the personal cleanliness of the Scholars." ('Lavatory' in the sense of running water).

Understaffing

Mr. Van appears to have worked hard in very trying conditions but was apparently not an organizer. He agonized over the misbehaviour of various boys, and tried other methods than the cane in order to make them promise to be 'better' boys. Most of the time he was seriously understaffed, with, it was acknowledged, very little in the way of quality teachers. The clergy came in to take Scripture quite often, the Drawing Master and Drill Sergeant came too, but none of these sources of help could be relied on. Clergy and Drawing Master took their holidays at different

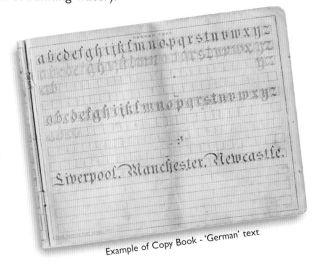

Example of Copy Book - 'German' text

times from the school, the Sergeant had expeditions to attend to and with no instant communication, the Master had to change the timetable when the help didn't arrive and amalgamate classes. Drill couldn't take place if the weather was bad because of the muddy surface of the playground and the road outside. The **Inspector** remarked that the boys were only orally good in Geography. It transpired that they had no books, knowledge improved after atlases and geography readers arrived. Mr. Van reported to the Managers that there wasn't proper accommodation for writing (in copy-books). No doubt slates could be propped on knees to write upon, but copybooks and paper would need desk support. A 'block of desks' was supplied later when they moved school.

In May **1882** an under-lined entry shows: "**P. T. Nicholls left to-day**." He had tried the patience of two Masters (who both gave him extra lessons to try to improve his work) he had squabbled with the Monitors, set a bad example and, reduced the education of a good number of boys. So after five years of scolding, coaxing and coaching, and having an incompetent trainee teacher before the classes, he left. However in the **Inspector's Report** of June, he stated that "C. W. Nicholls was now qualified under Article 79 [to teach]." So he could have taught elsewhere!

Bad air
On October 26th of that year, the Master makes an interesting entry regarding the sanitation situation: "The Vicar called. I have been obliged to stay at home till after school commenced each day, as the bad air has poisoned my blood like it did two years ago. I mentioned it to him and he said the alterations were to be made at once. The builder says it will be three weeks before things will be ready." The men came a month later to commence the alterations to the 'offices'.

The **Diocesan Inspector** reported: "The boys in Division I are so crowded that it is difficult to carry out the work either of Instruction or Inspection."

Mr. Van "terminated his employment" at the end of **1884** having spent his last week away through the illness of a relative. He writes: "The curates came". They evidently took charge of the school for the last week of term.

Appointment of Mr. William Neal
With the appointment of Mr. William Neal from January 1st 1885 a new, better and long chapter was begun in the history of the boy's school. His first entry in the Log states "The boys were impudent." However after this remark, throughout his tenure the easy discipline and good behaviour of the boys was regularly reported upon.

The Master obviously worked with authority, as by the 12th of January he was able to report that the school worked very quietly. (This in contrast to the Inspector's Report for 1884 that stated: "noisy teaching of the Classes hinders the Boys' progress in an appreciable degree.")

William Neal quickly examined the work of the boys and found one class who knew nothing of the geography they were supposed to have learned, and the work of the 1st Standard in very poor condition. He subsequently found the school pence to be greatly in arrears, the debt amounting to £1. 15. 9d.

Boys' School to move to St. Johns Street
The **Government Report** for the year ending **1884** stated: The managers contemplate an early arrangement of their schools. The Boys will be transferred to the premises now used by the Girls Department and the Infants will occupy the entire building in the Bewdley Road. A

new Girls' School will be erected near St. John's Church. These proposals seem sensible, and if the idea can be carried out in its entirety the schools will be benefited in no slight degree. The rooms now occupied by the Boys will need considerable alteration before they can be adapted to the purposes of an Infants' School. As premises for a Boys' school they are most inconvenient, and it really seems impossible to conduct a Boys' School efficiently in such wretched quarters."

Scarlet and Typhoid fevers
In **1885** Scarlet fever was still shown to be a scourge, but some parents were apparently anxious about examination results. Mr. Neal notes in May:

"Mrs. Wheeler brought her boy James, who is in the first Standard up to the school in a carriage. He has had the Scarlet Fever and is in such a frightfully weak state that he cannot possibly be present at the examination."

By September another scourge was in place in the form of Typhoid Fever, it also necessitated boys staying at home if the disease was in the house.

Exchange of desks
Mr. Neal agreed to have the desks from the Infant School and he was allowed 'five new boxes for the slates'. He had now a 'Certificated' teacher as assistant. (It entitled him to the title of Head Master.) The move to the old Infants' School appears to have been made in September, a new classroom had been promised but had not yet been built. There was a delay with the desks, as the Infants' School had not received their Kindergarten ones. When school commenced after Christmas two entrances had been bricked up and another door put in.

Catapults
In March **1886** Mr. Neal writes: "Mr. Smith the owner of the adjacent mill sent word about the boys breaking his windows with stones thrown from catapults."

In June the Master gave a half holiday so that the three Assistants and thirteen of the boys who were in the choirs could take part in the **Worcester Festival**."

The report in August stated: "During the holidays the walls of the new class room were raised up and it is now in course of completion." There were 278 names on the register and an average attendance of 239 in a week." Measles was prevalent and accounted for much of the non-attendance.
In October a partition was put in between the school and the new classroom that came into use on November 1st. Also in November the children attended a Tea and Entertainment on behalf of the **Sutton Road Mission Church** (This was the wooden church that preceded Holy Innocent's Church).

In July **1887** the Master wrote to the Vicar about the nuisance arising from a neighbouring pig-sty.

The **Government Report** for **1886/7** praised the improved accommodation and the standards of learning and discipline. "The state of the School reflects high credit on its vigorous young Master and his willing colleagues. The efficiency of the institution has improved wonderfully since it came under its present staff of teachers."

In February **1888** the snow was thick on the ground, thick enough for the boys not to attend church!

The Mayors' Magic Lantern
In September the Mayor wished to give a Magic Lantern entertainment to the boys.
In March **1891** "A lecture on '**Animal Sagacity**' was given in the Town hall by the [historian] **Rev. J. R. Burton** to the boys of Standards 4-7."

In April the assistant teachers, Mr. Powell and Mr. Gardner acted as enumerators in taking the census.

At the end of May **1892** a weeks' holiday was given for the reconstruction of the 'offices'. Two reasons for being thankful!

In June arrangements were made for the boys to have the use of the **swimming bath** in Mill Street for an hour on Mondays, two of the teachers were to teach them and the Vicar promised to assist.

Teachers Treat
In September the teachers drove to **Witley Court** (along with the teachers from the girls' school) there was a half-holiday for the occasion.
The **Government Report** that year made some criticisms with regards to subject attainment, but also reported: "Perfect discipline is maintained without any apparent effort. No steps have yet been taken to establish a Penny Bank and a Library in the school."

On the 22nd the teachers and pupils were present at the **Laying of the Foundation Stone** of the New North Aisle of **St. John's Parish Church**.

In **1893** the school received a surprisingly poor report from the **Diocesan Inspector**: "Many of the answers given were of a wild description." While there are reported "Visits from the Vicar." There are not the more customary reports of clergy taking classes for religious instruction.

The **Government Inspectors'** report also was not complimentary, though he did consider that the change of date of the Examinations and the change of teachers might be in part to blame. Mr. Neal himself cited the overcrowded state of classrooms and the excessive number of teachers and boys working in the schoolroom 60 boys regularly occupied the two small classrooms, which should have only contained 40 each. The noise prevented successful teaching there. Average attendance had been 330 for the last 5 weeks, the accommodation being for 301. He asked for an additional classroom and the division of the schoolroom.

Obviously playground equipment is not just a modern idea for in July the '**Pole of the Giant's Stride**' fell there was no injury to any of the boys. In August the partition in the Schoolroom had been put in place. The master commented that teaching was not now so laborious as formerly and was more effective. In December two small stoves were placed in the two smallest classrooms.

In July there was a half-holiday for the **Parish Social** gathering when about 50 of the boys were taking part in the Athletic Sports.

The **Inspector** that year reported: "overcrowding, obsolete desks and books in need of renewal hindering progress". Though in **1895** the Diocesan Report "showed further improvement."

The **Government Report** of that year showed considerable progress with the result that the coveted Higher Fixed Grant was awarded.

In **1897** the school gained a good report from the Inspector, but he added: "Better drainage is needed in the playground so that after rain the surface water may not remain in pools as at present."

Queen Victoria's Diamond Jubilee
On June 22nd the Queen's Diamond Jubilee Day, the boys had tea in school. They had a holiday the next day.

Insufficient gas light
In October a letter was written to the Managers stating the school was insufficiently lit by the gas. Mr. Larr examined the fittings the next day. In January next, nine incandescent burners were fixed in three of the rooms. No doubt these were an improvement on the previous ones, but gas lighting cannot have been very efficient in large rooms with high ceilings.

Kate Bywater was engaged to assist when Mr. Neal was ill for three months beginning in March **1898**. Her engagement was terminated in September 1899 when she went to Training College. (She subsequently succeeded Miss Catherine Bailey as Headmistress at **St. Mary's Girls' School** in 1904). Another assistant, Mr. W. Tipler also went to Training College at that time, the Managers had advertised 6 times for a replacement but had no applicants. Mr. Schwamenkruge had taken charge successfully in Mr. Neal's absence. The following year in March **1900** he was to leave the school to enter the service of the School Board in Birmingham. Leaving the Master without his chief Assistant.

A report of May 11th states: "G. Evans a former scholar of this school has obtained the **Brinton Medal**, the highest distinction at the local Grammar School."

Then on May 17th "**Mafeking** was relieved at 3 a.m. today, no school this afternoon."

The Government Report states: " skill and industry shown by the teachers. W. Tipler has obtained a First Class in the Queen's Scholarship Examination." There is obviously a change in the status of Pupil Teachers, for two are described as 'Old Style'.
"The return of 'Our Volunteers' from South Africa in June" warranted the closure of the school for the official 'Welcome Home'. This was followed in June **1902** by another holiday for the "Peace Rejoicings" in the town.

Salaries
In April **1903** the teachers' salaries were now to come from the Borough Education Committee. (See above when a boy had to be sent to collect them from the Managers.)

Urinal economies
An entry in June **1904** reads: "A new copper pipe has been placed in the urinals as the Education Committee has complained of our using 2600 gallons more than the quantity allowed us." (This was perhaps an economy to help with the teachers' salaries.)

Fireguards and pictures
In November **1905** there was an L. E. A. "Visit of inspection" Their report stated: "A fireguard is required for each stove in a school. There are two stoves at present unprovided with this protection." In February **1906** the Inspector endorsed their concern: "Two stoves need fireguards A supply of pictures would tend to brighten the rooms considerably." The guards were eventually provided in October.

New Boots

In December nine boys received new boots from the Police Boot Fund. A Rummage Sale was held in support of the fund.

In January **1907** the Inspector wrote that: "unsuitable desks should be replaced as soon as possible." In September **20 new dual desks** were received and also 4 incandescent burners were placed in the small classroom in place of 8 ordinary burners. However in February **1909,** the report stated: "Many of the desks are old and of a bad type, the seats being much too far from the desks the long stove pipes are contrary to regulations the cloakroom accommodation is inadequate." In June 115 desks were brought from the Infant school to replace some of the older desks.

'Boss Neal' with Standard 5 in the early 1900s

Courtesy Roy Bagnall

In October Mr. Dalley, Chairman and Miss Badland, Member of the Local Education Committee visited to inspect the dual desks. Mr Neal took the opportunity to show them some of his 'antiques'. He was asked to place a requisition order. He also had a problem with the Night School using the day school cupboard, and needed another.

In February **1910** he received **36 new dual desks** from Glasgow - 9 had broken castings and wood of one damaged. This was later remedied.

Board of Education Report of June 1910:

"The boy's school was originally built in 1850 for infants. The school is carried on in three separate buildings some distance from each other. On the whole a satisfactory building but not designed in accordance with modern ideas. 2 small front classrooms were over crowded on the 10 square ft. basis. Surface of playground should be formed of finer material now rough loose stones."

Central heating

In August **1911** 6 stoves and pipes were removed and a hot water apparatus was installed.

In **1912** the **Inspector** reported: "Boys are in excellent order.... The organisation of this Department cannot be considered satisfactory, as except for the help of a student teacher the Head Master is tied down with a large class and gets little opportunity to supervise the general work of the school and test the scholars progress."

In May the **Annual School Treat** took place it took the form of tea and school sports in a field near Sutton Park Road.

In May **1913** the playground was surfaced with gravel, and in August there was the first mention of a woodwork class.

Oversized classes

In September Mr Trahearne had a class of 58 boys, Mr Waite (Uncertificated) had Standards 3 & 1 combined, they numbered 80 boys. William Clarke had Standard 5 and part of Standard 7 equalling 49 boys, Mr Norledge 41 Standard 2 boys and the Head had 39 in Standard 4. Shortly after Mr. Waite had (not surprisingly) lost his voice so one of his classes was given to Mr Clarke while Mr Neal took one of Mr. Clarke's classes as well as his own.

The **Inspector's Report** of April **1914** drew attention to the crisis in staffing:

> "In two previous reports attention has been called to the defect in staffing this Department , and no extra Assistant teacher has been appointed to relieve the Head Master of charge of a large class, so that his functions are limited to those of a class teacher and he has no opportunity to control and supervise the instruction and discipline of the School. To make matters worse there is a vacancy on the staff and an Assistant Master has charge of Standards 2 & 5 numbering 80 boys on the books, which is a breach of Article 14 of the Code. Moreover a recent addition to the staff is only a temporary Certificated Teacher, who failed in his examination. - recent terms' examination papers shew falling off in attainments etc. - discipline is still good in spite of frequent changes of classes. Some loads of gravel have been put on the playground but it is "too coarse".

He also called upon the L.E.A. to explain their failure to provide proper cloakroom accommodation. The foregoing report was before the outbreak of World War I. 'Call-ups' of staff soon began to show their impact. In **1914** St. George's School was granted the loan of Mr George Jacobs from St. John's because of their teachers being called up for active service.

In **1915** an entry on the Log shows that a Health Centre had been established in 20 Lion Street. The **French Flag Day** was observed on July 14th when a procession took place to Brinton Park.

More staffing difficulties
By August "Mr. Trahearne was attempting to teach 81 boys of Standards 3 & 4. No additional teacher had arrived. Perhaps he felt some relief when he was called up for army service in October! Supply teachers came to replace Mr. Jacobs who was still at St. George's (though he was subsequently called up for active service) and Mr Harold Thomas Davison, then a Lieutenant on military duty. Increasingly women supply teachers were added to the staff when available.

At the end of May **1916**, Mrs. Evans, supply teacher and clerk to the school being absent, and Mr. Waite having taken 25 boys swimming, Mr. Neal records:

> "The teaching staff consists of two Mistresses both Uncertificated and myself, the afternoon passes very quickly if not pleasantly."

Coventry Street School having been closed by the Medical Officer of Health, an Uncertificated mistress was able to come to assist the next day. In cases where a teacher was sent to assist a school in even greater need, Mr. Neal had to amalgamate two classes, moving four boys to another class in order not to breach the code by having more than 60 in one class.

Tank Day
In April **1918** the boys attended a rehearsal, conducted by Mr. Evans in Bennett Street Council School for "Tank Day". On the day the children took part in a procession. The school had subscribed for 33 15/6d certificates for War Savings.

End of the War

The end of the war is not recorded in the Log Book for the school was closed because of the 'Spanish Flu' outbreak that cost so many lives. In January **1919** two of the male teachers returned to the school upon their discharge from the army. Mr Clarke who had been in charge of St. George's School since May 1916 also returned, but only for a month, when he was appointed to Lea Street Boy's School as Headmaster. There were still absences caused by the influenza.

Peace celebrations

Peace celebrations were delayed until July **1919**. On the 19th tea was partaken in the school, singing took place in front of the Corn Exchange followed by a procession to Brinton Park when some of the proceedings were stopped by rain. However the new flag and flagpole were used for the first time.

An entry in the Log Book for March **1920** reports:

"Mr. Jacobs (C.T.) who had contracted Enteric [fever] in Mesopotamia and spent some two years in hospitals, returned to school in November last. He remains in an enfeebled state, collapsed this morning, and was taken home."
He was subsequently pronounced unfit by doctors but carried on teaching. In **1922** some married women teachers services were dispensed with to make room for others.

Mr. Neal retired

On Feb 27th **1925** Mr. William Neal retired at the age of 62, after 40 years in the same post. In view of his success it is of interest to look at his personal history so far as it can be gleaned from the Census.

William Neal was aged 22 when he took over the school. He was listed as a lodger, living at 9 Summer Place, Kidderminster on the Census of 1891. He was born at Newark, Nottinghamshire, the son of a schoolmaster, and had trained at St. Peter's College, Peterborough. He was single when he arrived, but in spite of his strenuous efforts in school, he had found time to court Ada, for by 1901 he was married and had three small children, they lived at 32 St. Johns Street, near to the school. Some people will remember his son, a chemist, who kept the shop next to where Woolworth's store now stands in Worcester Street. He generously gave £100 for annual prizes to be given to the schoolchildren.

Gil Edwards went to the infants' school on the corner of Chapel Street in 1920 when Mrs. Bradburn was Headmistress. He says that most mornings the children had to line up and hold out their handkerchiegfs for inspection, anyone with dirty boots was given a brush and polish to get them cleaned, very few boys had dirty handkerchiefs of boots. He joined the boys' school in 1924, Mr. Neal's last year, he remembers him as being very strict. He was known as **Boss Neal**. On special days he would wear a top hat and tailcoat. The deputy Mr. **W.H. Trahearne** succeeded Mr Neal as Head Master. Gil says that he got him interested in arithmetic, which later got him into mathematics.

St. John's Infant Class photo 1923
Gil Edwards top row, 2nd from right

Mr. Trahearne was now responsible for the entries in the Log Book, these however were less revealing than those of his predecessors, as they were mostly concerned with absences, movements of teachers and annual holidays. When Mr. Stephen W. Miller B.A. was appointed at the same time he became the first teacher on the staff to hold a degree.

In March **1927** the **Inspector's Report** is somewhat critical of Mr. Trahearne's leadership, he considers that the fact that the master "had spent so many years on the assistant staff of the school - may perhaps be ascribed his failure to make any vital change either in the curriculum or in educational methods." Though he reports: "The discipline is good and the boys are responsive and are encouraged to develop without repression. The Head Master and his staff all work hard and in several respects good results are being obtained." In **1930** the Inspector still had the same kind of concerns.

St. John's Boy's Class 6 & 7 in 1938   Courtesy of Gil Edwards

School visits
The children however were enjoying trips to Kew Gardens and Windsor, London and Crewe in the early 30's. On the return from summer holidays in August **1932** the playground was found to be asphalted, in place of the former gravel.

In **1936** the late local historian **George Hall**, a pupil at the school was awarded a scholarship at King Charles I School.

Outbreak of war
In **1939** war was declared during the summer holiday in September causing the school to open a week late, the teachers, like their colleagues at the girls' school, had been busy receiving evacuees from Smethwick and arranging their billets.

Another 1938 class of boys in the classroom at the St. John's Street School - showing the glass partitions
Courtesy of Roy Bagnall

Staffing difficulties
By **1940** the school began to suffer staffing difficulties again with the call-up of Mr. S. Fletcher in January. There was already a shortage of supply teachers, there had been none available when the Head Master was ill in December. A teacher who was a Conscientious Objector, was granted exemption from military service and had to leave the school in July. Such people were not usually allowed to continue in their jobs but had to wear battledress uniform and do menial tasks often involving (I recollect) digging, around the country. The coke that heated the school ran out on the 23rd and the school had to be closed. It was the beginning of a particularly severe winter.

Air raid shelters

By September air raid shelters of brick and concrete had been constructed in the playground, the playground gate was to be kept unlocked so that people living in the neighbourhood could use the shelters at night.

New Senior Schools

At the end of September boys over eleven years of age were transferred to the new Senior Schools at Hurcott Road and Habberley Road. Mr. Miller went with the boys to Hurcott (**Sladen**) School), and Mr. Wridgway to Habberley (**Harry Cheshire**) School. This reduced the number of boys on roll to 86. Many of the boys had to carry desks from their previous school to the new one to save the new schools from being requisitioned by the army!

In May **1943** a part of the iron railings round the school were removed for salvage by instructions from the Ministry of Works

Staffing difficulties continued with often no supply teacher being available and the school reverted to having to borrow staff from other schools.

VE Day

On May 8th **1945** two days' holiday was given in celebration of the end of the war in Europe. **VJ Day** the end of the war in the East, came in August during the Summer Holiday. After it, Mr. Jacobs went for a course of treatment at Droitwich, he was evidently still suffering the effects of the Enteric Fever he caught during the first World War.

Mr. Trahearne retired, Mr. Miller made Head

Mr. W. H. Trahearne "terminated his engagement as Head Master" at the end of July **1946**. He had joined the staff as a Pupil Teacher from St. Mary's Boy's School in 1903, and gained his 'Certificate' in 1904. He had one break in service when he served in the army in WWI. Mr. S. W. Miller succeeded Mr. Trahearne. Mr Miller had already taught at the school before transferring to Sladen Senior School in 1940. He also, wrote sparingly in the Log Book, but as before there were full reports of their efforts at the School Music Festivals, conducted by Mr. Vaughan Williams and later by Mr. Benoy. Both these adjudicators were adept at praising the efforts while giving instruction for improvement.

Buildings and environment report

In **1949** His Majesty's Inspectors made a comprehensive report about the school buildings and environment. The report is a very lengthy one, because it describes very fully the building and situation. I have put a much fuller account than the one below as an appendix. Some extracts are given here:

> "The school buildings, erected in 1850, stand on the summit of a steep bank in the angle formed by the junction of the main roads from Shrewsbury and Bewdley to Kidderminster. [*The site lies somewhere underneath the Proud Cross roundabout on the Ring Road*] the 5 W.C's should all be kept in a satisfactory state of repair. One of them is at present derelict. There is no playing field easily accessible, the boys of the top class having to walk two miles to reach Aggborough playing field. Inside the main buildings, improvements could be made by the removal of old charts and framed prints and their replacement with attractive pictures. As soon as possible the old dual desks now in every classroom should be replaced with others of a more modern design. In one classroom no less than 6 of the desks are without backs."

Controlled status

On April 9th **1951** the school was granted Controlled status. During the summer holidays extensive alterations were made to the building, including the **installation of electricity**, repairs to the roof and frontage, interior decoration, lavatories being made self-flushing etc. In **1952** 102 boys were taken to London and enjoyed a " river trip and a visit to the Tower etc".

Birchen Coppice Junior School ready

In October Birchen Coppice Junior School was at last ready for occupation and 48 boys were transferred there with their teacher Mr. Gregory.

In **1953** "A disastrous fire, which wrecked the Parish Room", upset the school's dining arrangements and they had to serve dinners at the School.

At the **1955 School Prize-giving**, the prizes were presented by Mr. **George Jacobs**, the former teacher at the School who had survived World War I.

When the School re-opened after the summer holidays there were now only 84 boys on roll, with three teachers Mr. R. W. Vale, Mr. J. M. Billings and the Head Master. Mr. Vale moved to Comberton Junior School in July.

In **1957** and **1958** the school paid visits to **Carding Mill Valley** and **Malvern.**
In July **1959** the status of the school changed when St. John's Boys' and St. John's Girls' Schools became **St. John's Junior Mixed School**. However this did not mean that they were in one school building, there were many trials and frustrations before that was to come about.

ST. JOHN'S JUNIOR C. E. MIXED SCHOOL

Mr Jack Charles Hymas took over the Headship of the School on 1st September **1959** from Mr. Stephen Miller. The deputy Education Officer called later in September and mentioned that the Education Committee were still trying to get a new school built but it had not been sanctioned so far. A Managers' Meeting in November met and discussed Staffing, as the school was now overstaffed!

Telephones

In December a new telephone was installed in each school making contact easily available.

Head's Office/Staff room provided

In **1960** The removal of the equipment for the school meals service in St. John's Street School provided a room to be used both as Headmaster's office and a Staff room!

There had been so much **illness among the staff** that the schools performance at the Musical Festival had to be cancelled the children didn't know the songs well enough. Eight children were selected for grammar schools notwithstanding the re-organisation and sickness.

The school outing was to the **Tower of London** in June of that year, the next year it was to **Chester** and in 1962 they visited **London Airport**. Miss Duigan, the deputy head, resigned through ill health, her place was taken by Miss Nancy Gill.
In March **1962** Dr. Mathews, the Principal of Shenstone Training College, brought a party of students to help in the school, as two teachers were absent.

Chilblains

Mrs. Sandra Perrett joined the staff in May. She taught Class 2 in St. John's Street School. She remembers having to wear boots throughout the winter because of the draught that came through a two-inch gap at the bottom of the door causing her to have chilblains! In May Miss M. S. Tipper resigned because of continuing ill health, she had taught in the district for 32 years. The number on roll in September was now 165.

Mr Hymas resigned in December, he wrote: "Mr. J. C. Brooke (Worcestershire Director of Education) came to say goodbye to me, he was appreciative of all the good work done since the schools were reorganised "

In January **1963 Nancy Mary Gill** took over as Acting Head of the school until the appointment of a successor to Mr. Hymas. There was an extra class of infants, an overflow from Hume Street. Mr. Greaves had to move his class from Brook Street to the Hall at St. John's Street to make room for them, in order that the dining room could be kept as such. 120 children were having dinners every day. 202 children were on roll now. There were 7 teachers including the Head.

Frozen pipes

Later in the month there was no water coming into the kitchen, it was found that the pipes were frozen under the ground, the supply to the cloakroom was lost. Water had to be carried from a nearby house for washing up. The school had to be closed as the main was frozen in the street. On February 1ˢᵗ it was arranged that a supply of water to Brook Street would be brought from the main by polythene pipes. This severe cold weather was being experienced throughout the country and wasn't to abate until well
into March.

Spare Classrooms?

In February the H.M.I. visited looking for spare classrooms with a view to accommodating yet another class of infants. The only room not in use as a classroom was the Dining Room, which he thought could be used. This would have made arrangements for dinner very difficult with 120 children taking them. Another Infants class was to come to Brook Street after Easter, some dinners were to be served in the Church Hall. Food was to be sent from both the Franche and Central kitchens.

Mr. G. M. Meredith appointed

On September 1ˢᵗ Mr. Meredith assumed the headship with Miss Gill as deputy.
Three classes of 7 and 8 years old children were to be at Brook Street School with three teachers, Miss Gill being in charge. 3 classes of 8 to 10 years old children were to be at St. John's Street School. School dinners were to be taken in the Parish Hall.

Naughty boys

In October naughty boys let off fireworks in the cloakrooms of Brook Street School, taking advantage of it being open in the evening before the Girl Guides arrived.

Visits

The Playhouse theatre was visited in November, in order to see *Mango Street Magic*. Mrs. Perrett took three parties of children to **Minster Carpet Works** the same month. In spite of all the difficulties the children were taken to shows quite regularly, they went to the Parish Hall in 1964 to see *The Trial,* and in 1966 *Toad of Toad Hall* at Shenstone College'

There were so many children now that there had to be two Christmas parties at Brook Street.

Shortage of chairs and tables unfixed radiators

1964 started with 34 children from Hume Street being placed in the spare classroom at Brook Street. Chairs and tables for the extra children having dinners, had not arrived, when they did they were the wrong size! Two radiators had been fixed to the walls but not joined to the heating system.

Bag counting

An argument ensued about the coke deliveries, having no resident caretaker counting the number of bags delivered would necessitate a teacher leaving a class to count them!

In April, a new **rotary ink duplicator** was delivered.

An extra 80 children

There was a great turnover of staff at this time through retirement and other reasons. In December the Head was advised that he should expect an extra 80 children at the school. He asked for the removal of a large stock cupboard from room 3W to 4D to give the teacher more room.

No alterations done - dangerous boiler

In **1965** the school opened without the alterations to the scullery in Brook Street being carried out. The repairs scheduled for St. John Street School had not been undertaken, and were still awaited at the end of April. An escape of steam from the boiler there proved that it was in a dangerous state. The thermometer was 50 degrees in error. Medical inspections had to be carried out in the Parish Hall. At this time teachers interviewed for posts at the school appear to have quite regularly withdrawn their acceptance upon reflection.

The children visited Stratford, Warwick and Coventry, with tea at a restaurant. The trip had been planned for months, with much preparation.

D. I. Y.

The St. John's School boiler developed a leak during the summer holidays and had been taken out but had not been replaced. Screens ordered for the large room, (to make more classrooms) were not ready and substitute screens arrived which Mr. Meredith had to bolt and assemble - they were very inconvenient. There were now 275 children on roll, (85% stayed to dinner) and eight teachers plus the Head, two of the classes were over forty in number, with one class of nineteen for slower children. The Dinner Lady staff was experiencing regular replacement. The screen that had failed to arrive had not yet been ordered. In October the boiler was leaking again.

Arrival of screens

In November the Head drew attention to the large increase in the size of the school and the need for more teaching space next September when the numbers were likely to be well over 300. He also asked that the new main to the Brook Street toilets should be installed as quickly as possible. Later that month the new screens arrived three to divide the large room at Brook Street and one to make a teaching corner at St. John's Street.

In January **1966** the teaching staff met at St. John's Street to view the sketch plan of the new buildings to be built in Blakebrook. In March the boiler in St. John's Street was continuing to leak.

By June there was still delay in the commencement of building the new school. Mr. Prosser the new building inspector advised that an office was to be erected in the St. John's Street playground and hoped it would be before the end of term. It was also hoped to install the new water main....

Death on a school trip
On July 1st there is an unusually sad Log Book entry:

> "On Friday 1st July Mr. Walbeoff collapsed and died whilst on an educational visit to Chester. --- Whilst waiting admission to the King Charles' Tower Mr. Walbeoff suddenly fell, pitched through the rails to the foot of the wall, some eight feet. The Rev. John Willis and Miss Gill clambered down the wall to him but he was inert. --- There was no indication of life. I asked Miss Gill to take the party to Chester Zoo and stayed by Mr. Walbeoff with Mr. Willis. A post mortem examination was carried out on Saturday and the pathologist has reported that death was caused through coronary thrombosis."

After that sad and dramatic event mundane frustrations had to be dealt with: - " there is no hope of receiving either the office hut at St. John's Street, nor the storage shed at Brook Street [for storage and cleaning materials]. I am unable to make arrangements with the cleaner and unable to receive deliveries of furniture for the class which is to occupy the present staff-room. "Telephone call to Worcester revealed the failure by the office to order the new piano promised for September. This is essential to permit music teaching in the new term." Hope must have returned with the news that "work began on the 4th July on the new buildings."

THE NEW BUILDINGS

Mr. **G. M. Meredith**, the new head found that the hut had been erected in the playground of St. Johns Street School, to serve as an office, but not fitted, the previous administrative room had been fitted out for a small class, but transfer of the materials could not take place - all the furniture had not been delivered.

Five classes were now housed at Brook Street and five at St. John's Street. By September a phone had been fitted in the hut. A piano had been delivered to Brook Street, but the defective boiler, reported last September was now being dismantled at St. John Street. In October it was reported that the boiler had not been mended and it was cold. It was patched up a week later.

Two coaches of children went on a well prepared for outing to Caer Caradoc and Clun. At Christmas the Nativity service by the children was improved by the use of a **microphone and amplifier.**

BLAKEBROOK

On September 4th 1967 St. John's (C. E.) commenced school in the new buildings, at Blakebrook though many parts of the buildings including the upstairs toilets and the apparatus in the kitchen were not yet functioning. Items not yet delivered included the desks for the teachers, piano for the Hall and wireless equipment. There were now seven classes of Juniors. 90 new pupils came on the first day. By the 9th, the telephone had still not been connected. The new piano was delivered on the 20th. By the end of the month it was found that the Infant school was in great difficulties with regard to accommodation and would need the prefabricated classroom for the summer term.

By February **1968** the Brook Street buildings were made available for the summer term. Various alterations were to be made to the building. The news of the use of Brook Street buildings was received badly by the parents who had expressed their delight at the new building. It was arranged that in April classes should spend morning or afternoon at Brook Street. It was considered that pressure upon accommodation was likely to be prolonged indefinitely. Urgent consideration should be given to the erection of prefabricated classrooms at Blakebrook to avoid the grave educational and social disadvantage of a split primary school.

In July another well-planned trip took place to Ludlow, Stokesay Castle, the Llanfair Light Railway and Powis castle. There was a Recorder Festival at Blakebrook with Mr. Benoy conducting, later in the month when 6 schools visited, some classes had to be sent to Brook Street to avoid congestion.

In September the school opened with **348 children** in the school. Now two classes were permanently based at Brook Street and seven at Blakebrook.

At Christmas 400 parents attended the Christmas carol service, use was made of an amplifier, tape recorder and three speakers.

New temporary classrooms were expected for January **1969**. It was decided that the Brook Street School would then become a **Teachers' Centre**.

At the beginning of January parts of two classrooms were delivered though it was thought that the Borough Planning Authority had refused permission. Two halves were left on the site and playground.

The year had begun with several teachers absent, by February the school had two supply teachers with the office having exhausted its list of them. Miss Wright was still away as a result of her accident. The two classes moved back from Brook Street as the new classrooms had at last been erected.

All together
September 1969 360 on roll 11 classes on one campus.

Re-organization took place four years later in **1973** when the three-tier system was imposed upon the area. This was to be reversed in **2006** when the two-tier system was again the chosen method of division. The new arrangements were implemented in 2007.

APPENDIX

The H. M. I.'s Report on Buildings: (1946)

"The School buildings erected in 1850, stand on the summit of a steep bank in the angle formed by the junction of the main roads from Bewdley to Kidderminster . The immediate neighbourhood is closely packed with small dwellings of the artisan type, mainly co-eval with the School itself. What was originally the main hall of the building has been divided into two classrooms by a glazed partition. (The larger of the two rooms thus formed, measuring about 30' x 25', is able to accommodate all the boys at morning assembly.) Abutting this main room on the south side are one classroom and a cloakroom, on the north side are two small rooms each measuring 20' x 16', one used as a classroom and the other as a dining room and scullery combined. One hundred and twenty eight boys grouped in 4 classes according to age were in attendance at the time of the Inspection. Buildings erected so long ago naturally have many deficiencies when judged by modern standards, but much can be done to make them more suitable as an environment in which young boys can develop happily and freely in mind and body. The exterior of the building has long had a most depressing appearance, but a new coat of paint applied during the summer holidays has made a welcome improvement. Floors in two of the small rooms have been replaced, the many holes in the surface of the playground have been filled in, and the offices cleaned and whitewashed; but much more remains to be done. On the north side flanking St. John's Street, two narrow strips of ground intervene between the classrooms and the playground. The railings enclosing these strips were removed during the war, with the result that the ground has become a mere dust patch. If some kind of fencing could be replaced here, shrubs, flowers or grass might be planted once more. There is also a small patch of ground on the east side, which offers possibilities as a small school garden. The offices can never be made really satisfactory short of complete reconstruction, but the 5 W. C's should all be kept in a satisfactory state of repair. One of them is at present derelict. A wire basket should be provided in the playground for waste papers, and a few seats under the tree would be welcomed by the children. There is no playing field easily accessible, the boys of the top class having to walk about two miles to reach borough playing field. Such a long walk is not only fatiguing for such young children but is expensive of time; field games under such conditions can hardly be a justifiable use of school time, and efforts might be made to secure the use of a ground nearer to the School. Much can be done to make the cloakroom a more attractive and suitable place. The removal of one of the coat racks and the adaptation of the remainder has been suggested to the Head Master. The various impediments should be removed to the Caretaker's store. The two washbowls provided are inadequate for 128 boys; considerable extra provision is desirable even if of a temporary nature. The three roller towels, now laundered once weekly, should be replaced more frequently, and individual towels provided as soon as opportunity offers. Inside the main buildings, improvements could be made by the removal of old charts and framed prints and their replacement by attractive pictures. As soon as possible, the old dual desks now in every classroom should be replaced by others of a more modern design. In one classroom no less than 6 of the desks were without backs, and several others were so unsuitable that the feet of the children using them were within 6" of the ground. --- The supply of reading and reference books throughout the school is poor. Many of the older books are in a dilapidated state and should be scrapped.

The boys attending this school come from St. John's Infant school at the age of 7, and   partly from Birchen Coppice Temporary School at the age of 8. The latter children are kept for the extra year at the Infant's School because of the acute pressure on the accommodation of the Junior Schools in the area. Now that the new Birchen Coppice Primary School is included in the building programme for 1950 this undesirable situation should be somewhat eased. Transport is provided for the Birchen Coppice children (at present about 40)."

PLACES

Aldershot 13, 14
Bastille 27
Bewdley 20, 26
Bewdley Hill 15
Bewdley Street (Road) 17, 18, 19, 26, 27, 34, 72, 75
Birchen Coppice 70
Birchen Coppice Junior School 71, 84
Birmingham 7
Blackwell Street 20
Blakebrook 19, 25, 26, 35, 39
Blakebrook Cottage 29
Blakebrook County Hospital 28
Blakebrook House 27, 37
Bradford 12
Brinton Park 1-6, 32, 46, 56, 58, 66, 81
Bromsgrove Street 12
Brook Street 34, 71, 85, 86, 88
Broseley 62
Brussels Street 15, 16
Caldwell 26
Caldwell Castle 9, 55, 62
Canal Wharf 18
Carpet Hall 15
Castle Street 9
Cemetery 27
Cemetery Row 18
Chapel Street 19, 27, 32, 34, 38, 39, 43, 61
Chester Road 62
Chlidema Carpet Works 54
Church Street 27
Churchfields 20
Cobden Street 26
Comberton 31
Comberton Hill 4
Coventry Street School 33, 49, 80
Crowther Street 20
Cussfield 19
Dower House 29
Drayton House, Belbroughton 8
Eyemore Wood 40
Farfield Cottage 8
Foley Park Mixed School 63
Franche 33, 35
Franchise Street 17
General Hospital 28
George Street 4
Grand Turk Villas 28
Greenhill Farm 20
Habberley Road Schools 68, 83
Habberley Street 35
Habberley Valley 37, 40
Harry Cheshire School 33
Harvington Hall 50, 57
Hemming Street 26
Hill Street 15, 16
Hobro, Wolverley 49
Holman Street 17, 26
Hume Street 17, 34, 61
Hume Street Board School 43
Kidderminster Modern School 33
King Charles Grammar School 21
Larches Auxiliary Hospital 30
Larches Road 29, 33
Lea Street Girl's School 56
Lea Street School 61
Leamington 13
Leswell 22
Lisle Avenue 33
Lodge Pool 26
Malvern Sanatorium 59
Mill Street 18, 49, 51, 77
Minster Carpet Works 85
Moor Hall 8
Mount Skipett 15, 19
Neville Avenue 33
Oaklands House 12
Old Cemetery 25, 26

Old Pound 26
Old Square 19, 20
Park Lane 17, 18
Park Street 9, 15, 16, 22, 26
Paternoster Row 20
Peel Street 16, 26, 34
Plimsoll Street 26
Prospect Hill (School Clinic) 55
Ragged School 72
Redstone Caves 59
Reservoir 33
Rock Terrace 16, 19
Roman Catholic Chapel 25
Shubbery House 8
Sladen School 68, 83
Smethwick 33, 82
South Africa 50
Spring Bank, Leswell 12
St. Ambrose School 73
St. George's Church 25
St. John's Avenue 33
St. John's Church 25, 76, 77
St. John's Street 34, 35, 38, 71, 75, 81, 85-87
St. John's Terrace 72
St. Mary's Boys' School 83
St. Mary's Church 25
Stourport 31
Summer Hill 22, 72
Summer Hill House 54
Summer Place 24, 35, 81
Sutton-Suduuale 15
Sutton Common 28
Sutton Lane 1
Sutton Park Road 30, 31
Sutton Road 2, 3, 27, 28, 29
Talbot Street 3, 6, 17
The Battery 20
The Butts 18
The Larches 29
The People's Park 1
Tickenhill 51
Treatment Centre 28
Trinity Lane 29
Union Workhouse 25, 27
Washington Row 17, 29
Washington Street 28
Wood Street 9, 16, 24, 26, 27
Woodfield 24, 26
Woodfield Crescent 26
Woodfield Farm 25, 26
Woodfield House 20, 21, 26
Workhouse 47

PEOPLE

Addenbrooke, Mrs. S.H. 54
Addenbrooke, Miss. 65
Alford, Alice 44, 46
Badland, Miss. 79
Bailey, Catherine M. 35, 40, 49, 78
Baldwin, Miss. E. 35
Baldwin, Miss. M 37
Barker, Miss. 54
Barth, Arthur 73
Barth, Miss. 63
Bateman, Charles 14
Batham, Mr. 27
Baxter, Rev. Richard 30
Baxter, Richard 41
Baynes, Mrs. 54
Benn, Tony 14
Bennett, Councillor Henry 26
Bennett, Supt. 52
Benoy, Mr. 71, 88
Beswick, A. 72, 73
Billings, Mr. J.M. 84
Bishop, Sylvia 28
Bond, Nell 30

Bowie, Miss. 46
Boycott, William 24
Boyle, Mr. 72
Bradley, Benjamin 29
Bradley, George 29
Brancker, Rev. P.W. 43
Breakspear, Miss. 44
Bridges, Harry 5
Brinton, Brenda 8
Brinton, Henry 7, 8, 24
Brinton, John Chaytor 10
Brinton, John 1-10, 19
Brinton, Joshua 8
Brinton, Madeline 8
Brinton, Margaret 8
Brinton, Mary 8
Brinton, Oswald Waiter 10
Brinton, Reginald 8, 10
Brinton, Robert Percival 10
Brinton, Selwyn John Curwen 8
Brinton, William 7, 8, 19
Bristow, Mr. 24
Broad, Mr. 12
Broadfield, Edward 18
Brooks, Allan 26
Brooks, Ken 33
Broom, Mr. 24
Broome, F.C. 7
Broome, Sarah 8
Browning, Maria 13
Burton, Mary Haynes 41
Burton, Rev. John R. 34, 77
Butcher, George 29
Butcher, Mrs. 5
Butler Best, Emily & Cecilia 37
Butler Best, William 18, 37
Bywater, Kate 49, 78
Carter, Louisa 15
Caswell, Emily 40
Chalk, Harry 72
Chamberlain, Neville 66
Chambers, Dorothy 52
Chartist's 24
Cheshire, Harry 62
Churchill, Winston 69
Clark, Miss. 48
Clarke, Elizabeth 43
Clarke, Mr. 81
Clarke, William 79
Claughton, Vicar, Dr. 22,
Clewes, William 17
Clinton, Norman 14
Cockin, Rev. W. 20
Cooper and Brinton 7
Cope, Agnes 42
Cox, Miss. 53
Crane, William 15
Crayshaw, Captain 52
Dalley, Mr. 79
Davidson, Harold Thomas 80
Davies, Walford 65
Derricot, Madeline 42
Doulton & Co. 12
Downes, Miss. 46. 49
Dredge, Charles J. 16
Duce, Mr. 5
Duigan, Miss. 84
Duke of York 59
Dyer, Elsie 5
Ebury, Inspector 43
Eddy, Mayor E.G. 66
Eddy, Sir George 5
Edwards, W. H. 6
Edwards, Eleanor 49
Edwards, Gil 1
Edwards, Miss. 64
Eginton, Harvey 21
Evans, Mr. G. 78
Evans, Mr. 80
Evans, Mrs. 80

PUBLIC HOUSES